BISON
BOOKS

WEDDED

to the Game

THE REAL LIVES

OF NFL WOMEN

Shannon O'Toole

UNIVERSITY OF NEBRASKA PRESS § LINCOLN & LONDON

Publication of this book was assisted
by a grant from the Virginia Faulkner
Fund, established in memory of Virginia
Faulkner, editor in chief of the University
of Nebraska Press.

☾

Library of Congress Cataloging-in-
Publication Data
O'Toole, Shannon.
Wedded to the game : the real lives of
NFL women / Shannon O'Toole.
    p. cm.
ISBN-13: 978-0-8032-8625-2 (pbk. : alk. paper)
ISBN-10: 0-8032-8625-2 (pbk. : alk. paper)
1. Football players' spouses—United
States—Interviews. 2. Wives—Effect
of husband's employment on—United
States. 3. Football players—United
States—Family relationships.
4. National Football League. I. Title.
GV959.5.O76 2006
796.332'092'2—dc22
2005022112

Typeset by Kim Essman.
Designed by A. Shahan.
Printed by Edward Brothers, Inc.

To John and Tierney Rose Morton, with love

CONTENTS

ILLUSTRATIONS

PREFACE

The freshly painted white-walled house was quiet. Our German shepherd, Keisha, settling in to her new surroundings, had claimed the sunniest corner of the kitchen's linoleum floor for her afternoon snooze. I was making dinner, and as I carefully scooped vegetable clippings into a paper bag, Keisha jerked her head upright and began to bark. I also heard the car engine out front, but I said to her, "No, no, it's too early to be John."

It was only two o'clock, and John wasn't due home until after five (and usually later than that). Six weeks ago, and one week into the regular season, John had been signed to the Green Bay Packers' practice squad as a receiver. This was his second chance to play football in the NFL, after having been cut that summer at the end of training camp by the then Los Angeles Raiders, and he was determined to make it. If that meant being the first guy on the field in the morning and the last one to leave it at night, that was what he was going to do.

Not only that, but it looked like the Packers really wanted him. At first overwhelmed by the extensive playbook, John was beginning to feel at ease, and he would come home from practice energized and excited. His receiver coach, Jon Gruden, was especially positive about John's future and told him he might even be activated from the practice squad to the active roster by midseason. Learning from one of the best, Sterling Sharpe, John thought things had finally "clicked" and that he had found the place where he could grow and improve until the day he eventually became a starter.

This was why I had decided less than a month before to give up my full scholarship to Western Michigan University—and interrupt my studies in sociology—to join John in Green Bay. We were in love, and we had spent that summer together in Los Angeles—rollerblading at Manhattan Beach, riding horses in the Hollywood hills, and getting a taste for the NFL and what it might be like to share our lives together. In fact, nearly every moment in our then ten-month relationship had been amazingly exciting—an emotion that was probably heightened by our uncertain future—and it looked and felt like every midwestern girl's dream.

Perhaps the hardest part of my decision to move to Green Bay was telling my parents. I am their eldest daughter, and I was the first in the family to attend college. At that point, they hardly knew John at all, but for him I seemed ready to give up everything I'd worked so hard to achieve. That wasn't how I saw it, but when I left my parents' home in rural Michigan to drive to Green Bay, we all felt like we were in mourning. Despite my resolve, I wiped a near-constant stream of tears from my eyes during the entire eight-hour drive.

How could I explain to them how bored and lonely I'd become without John? How much I'd come to almost dread the new semester? A year ago my studies and my college softball career were completely satisfying, and now my thoughts continually wandered to John and all the fun and activity he was going through as he got settled in with the Packers. Our phone conversations had become heart-wrenching, ending in impassioned "Good-bye's" and "I miss you's." Marriage was the furthest thing from my mind—that was way too much commitment—but I began to seriously consider how John's goals and my aspirations could be meshed successfully.

And one thing that I'd always craved was the kind of life it seemed we might lead in the NFL. It wasn't the money that energized me. It was the adventure—the travel and unique experiences it seemed to offer. Ever since adolescence, I'd grown up cringing at the thought of a predictable, scheduled life nestled in the cornfields of mid-Michigan. Now I was twenty years old, miles away from the man I loved, and beginning to wonder how long I would wait for life to begin. My biggest fear was someday saying, "I wish I had. . . ."

From the beginning, almost from our first date, John turned the NFL into "our dream." He included me and wanted me involved in all the pro football excitement, and because of him, I became excited about it too. When his agent came to town, John invited me to join them for dinner. When John heard encouraging news about his chances of being drafted, I was the first person he called. Every day seemed to bring something new, but during all the hype, John always made me feel valued and important. Plus, we were clearly involved in something special and unique—none of our friends had ever experienced anything like this.

I wanted to see him reach his goals. I wanted to help him get "his shot." As a fellow athlete, I was proud when he asked me to train with him. I timed him in the 40, ran next to him down the snow-covered streets of Kalamazoo, and mixed protein shakes with him. We did everything together.

That afternoon, as I looked out the window to see who in fact had driven up, I found John getting out of his brand-new, two-toned Chevy blazer.

"It *is* him! I wonder if he's sick?" I asked out loud, glancing down at the dog as I wiped my hands on a dish towel.

I pushed open the kitchen door, a welcoming but questioning smile on my face. John didn't even acknowledge me but brushed past with his head down. He slunk onto a kitchen chair and faced the wall, leaving me to stare at the back of his green-and-gold sweatshirt. This can't be good, I thought blankly.

Still not facing me, he mumbled something about a meeting with someone in Packer personnel. "Guys are hurt. Needed to make room for some offensive linemen." Speaking only in fragmented phrases, his message vaguely began to penetrate. "Said he had to let me go. They appreciate all my hard work."

Suddenly he turned, and I saw that his mouth had twisted into a weird grin. Peering directly at me, he spat out, "They just cut me."

I didn't reply. I thought, "If he's smiling, then he must be joking."

Seconds went by as I incredulously searched his face. Then panic set in. I thought, "Oh God, he's not joking. It really happened. This is really happening." My throat tightened, and then the sensation of suffocation moved into my gut.

"What do you mean?" I said, my voice rising. "But your coaches!? They said you were doing a great job. I thought they liked you!"

"I don't know. They needed to make room on the roster. He called it 'a numbers game.'"

My gaze fixated on the still unpacked boxes lining the kitchen counter, so that I hardly noticed as John left the room and began shuffling through his address book. Then, with frustration and worry in his voice, I heard him say, "I need to call my agent."

No. This wasn't supposed to happen. I'd given up a full ride scholarship at a Division I college! I couldn't get that back. Green Bay was supposed to be our new home. Everything had been falling into place. But without his football salary, we couldn't live in this house. We couldn't afford half the things we'd just bought. Where would we go? Could I face moving home and living with my parents after this? And what would John do? Would we even be able to stay together?

Less than four weeks. I'd been there less than four weeks. I had said good-bye to my old life less than four weeks ago.

That night John and I lay in bed side by side, but I don't remember talking much or comforting each other. Curled onto my side and staring at the still unadorned bedroom wall, my mind reeled in disbelief. Our moving boxes would never be unpacked. We'd have to break our lease, and tomorrow I'd have to rummage for merchandise receipts and beg store managers to take returns. But most of all, the thought of calling home to Saginaw was making me sick to my stomach. Shit, what are we going to do?

In hindsight, John was naïve to think he would have a long, prosperous playing career in the NFL, since only 8 percent of undrafted rookies ever make an NFL roster. However, even if John had heard that dismal statistic, he would not have been deterred. Optimistic, single-minded, and determined, that's my John.

He wanted that exciting NFL life, too. John truly believed that the Packers' signs were pointed in the right direction, and I had no reason not to believe him. We both had faith that if you studied diligently (in this case, learned the playbook), then sweat, toiled, and gave 110 percent, success would follow. Isn't that what everyone's taught? The Packers had already praised John's attitude and work ethic, so staying on the team didn't seem to be a question.

I should have taken the first Raiders' release last summer as a warning of things to come, or at least as a clue of how the "Not-For-Long" League actually works. With the Raiders' roster already packed with talented veteran receivers, we simply blamed John's being cut on bad timing. Because John was already acclimated to cold-weather games—having gone to college at Western Michigan University as well—we told ourselves John was better suited for Green Bay anyway.

As I lay in bed that night, my feelings of desperation and shock turned to anger. I had just made one of the toughest decisions of my young life, and for what? So the NFL could mislead us and undo everything? I wasn't mad at John. I knew he had done ten times more than what was expected. It was those people.

Why did these teams elevate his hopes, applaud him as he spilled his blood working toward their vision, only to dispose of him weeks later? Did they have any idea how many people had been affected by their "numbers game"?

They're all the same, I thought. Liars. I hate them. I'll never trust the NFL again.

This book is about what it's really like to live inside the NFL, told from the unique perspective of the wives and girlfriends of pro football's players and coaches. Part insider tell-all and part sociological study, this book is packed with no-holds-barred, firsthand accounts of NFL life, providing a rare glimpse into the often hidden world behind the game. If you want the inside scoop on what the highly competitive, sometimes brutal, only rarely glamorous NFL is all about, just ask the women who live it every day.

Far from the stereotypical, fluffy Barbie doll image under which NFL wives often suffer, NFL women are sharp, strong-willed, and opinionated—and not afraid to speak their minds. Rather than being shallow or timid, as they are sometimes portrayed, they are as tough, if not tougher, than the men who play and coach the game. They have to be. Those who aren't don't last in the NFL for long, while those who learn to cope with the NFL's immense difficulties and challenges become stubborn, resilient, wise survivors.

Indeed, when head coach Steve Mariucci of the Detroit Lions was once asked by a reporter, "What is the most difficult position in pro football?" he replied: "Coaches' wives. For seven months during football season our wives are everything: teachers, cooks, counselors, nurses, moms, chauffeurs, you name it. These women have the most difficult job in pro football by far."

What is it like to stand by completely helpless as your boyfriend or husband is cut by teams, not once or twice, but a dozen times? How do relationships survive the stress, strain, and insecurity of that kind of life? What is it like to watch a Sunday game on television when it's your husband who can't get up from the turf? How do you keep your composure when, while sitting in a stadium, seventy thousand fans are screaming for your husband's head because of a dropped pass or poor play-calling?

What is it like to raise kids in the constant shadow of their NFL father? How do you deal with infidelity and domestic violence when the media are praising your football husband as a hero? How do you make friends or even think about having a career when you're moving with your husband's next job every year or two? When you're the one in the relationship always making the sacrifices and having your needs overlooked "for the good of the team," how do you *not* become hopelessly cynical and depressed? How, indeed, do NFL women maintain their sense of self, much less their sanity, while their husbands are employed by America's greatest game?

I must admit, when I began my research for this book I had an ulterior motive. Although I have been in the NFL for twelve years now and I know very well what this life is like, I was also seeking the advice and hard-earned wisdom of women who had already found solutions to my numerous concerns. I still struggle with this life I've chosen, and so I wanted to know: How do other women deal with the NFL? How do they cope and survive? What are their experiences?

To find out, I sent an anonymous survey to over 150 women and got back an amazing 75 responses. In most surveys, a 30 percent response rate is considered very good; 50 percent is unheard of. This surprised me more than anything: the eagerness of these women to talk—and not just about the good times, but about some of their most dreadful and unbearable experiences. NFL women are almost universally overlooked by the public and the media, and what I discovered is that they have things to say and they want to be heard.

Out of those 75 responses, I chose 30 women to interview in depth. Their stories make up the heart of this book. About half were willing to go on record and let their names be used, and about half wanted to remain anonymous. The reason for anonymity should be obvious. With their husbands still employed in a game where public image is everything, they didn't want to cause trouble, or risk their partners' jobs and livelihood, by speaking freely—and to speak freely is something they very much wanted to do. Occasionally, a fake name and profile have been created to hide a woman's identity; when this is done, it's noted in the text.

Who are the women you will meet? They range in age from their early twenties to their mid-sixties. In terms of educational back-ground, they range from high school graduates to women with advanced degrees and PhDs. Ethnically, most of the women identi-fied themselves as either African American or Caucasian, and each group made up about half of all respondents.

While some women said they worked outside the home, the ma-jority were full-time caregivers to small children. Of the women who had careers, job titles included clinical researcher, actress, artist, cosmetologist, substitute teacher, engineer, veterinary worker, ath-letic director, business development coordinator, nurse, social worker, travel director, and therapist/counselor.

The women in this book represent a wide range of tenures in the league. These ranged from two years—the girlfriend of a rookie free agent—to twenty-six years—the wife of a veteran defensive coordinator. The majority of respondents were married, while the rest were cohabiting and in a committed relationship.

In the initial anonymous survey, I asked respondents to either "agree strongly, agree mildly, disagree mildly, or disagree strongly" to a myriad of statements regarding NFL life. These responses form the basis of some of my general statements and conclusions about what off-the-field NFL life is like for women (and also often for men). The survey included nine pages of questions, among which the following were typical: "Because his job is so huge, sometimes it is difficult for me to carve out my own identity"; "As an NFL woman, I feel more pressure to have a great body and be sexy"; "The threat of [the player's/coach's] being cut–fired–released places considerable strain on our relationship."

A number of women did more than check boxes; they scribbled explanations and further thoughts in the margins and on the backs of pages, wherever they could. Then, over the course of my thirty one-on-one interviews, I received full, in-depth answers to these often difficult, complex questions. The voices brought forth in the interviews were extremely varied, but as often as not, their tone tended to reflect the number of years each woman had spent in the league. Often, women relatively new to pro football expressed optimistic enthusiasm for NFL life. Everything was still exciting, and their partners' futures were bright. Veteran wives were less inclined to cheerful optimism. They were comfortably relaxed and matter-of-fact and sometimes, not surprisingly, perhaps cynically resigned to the ways of NFL life.

I found that there is no typical NFL experience among women or families. The league's widely differing salaries, each player's or coach's level of fame (or anonymity), and the number of years in the NFL all greatly influence how people live, how they experience the NFL, and what issues they face. However, all of the women profiled in this book have one common characteristic: strength. They may not have started out tough and resilient, but the NFL has made them that way. Some of these women don't even know, or recognize, their own strength, but it's there, overshadowed by the names of their husbands or boyfriends in the sports pages.

Chances are, until their partners have played that last down or coached that final game, NFL women will be calling on that strength again and again. One NFL season might offer sunny skies, an endless string of "W's," and a trip to the Super Bowl, while the next year could bring nothing but losses, gloomy playoff predictions, and weekly media beatings. There are only two sure things about life in the NFL: it's often uncertain, and it's always exciting.

ACKNOWLEDGMENTS

To God, for all the blessings bestowed.

To my partner, my lover, and my best friend, John Morton. I am eternally grateful for the incredible support he has given me throughout this entire writing experience. No matter the obstacles, difficulties, and disappointments I faced, he never let me go "in the tank." I know that without his incredible coaching and motivational skills, this book would not have been written. Everything I know about perseverance and dedication to one's goals, I learned from him. I thank him for being my role model.

To Tierney Rose, our noble leader, for inspiring me every day.

To several special NFL women who encouraged and believed in this project from the beginning: Kim Ruddy, Pat Kennan, Kori Shaw, Gina Nedney, Julianne Player, and Lori Warhop. They spoke to others on my behalf and were always available to answer my many questions. I am extremely fortunate to have had such a fabulous group of women on my team. My deepest gratitude and appreciation to all.

To the other NFL women, named and unnamed, in this book and to women throughout the league: they have been my mentors, my sisters, and my friends, and I have learned important life lessons from each. Their incredible stories of strength and fortitude inspired me to tell our stories. Thank you for being the women you are.

To the University of Nebraska Press for the opportunity, and to my incredibly talented and hard-working developmental editor, Jeff Campbell, in San Francisco. His direction and guidance have been invaluable. From one Grinder to another, Thank you!

To my writing group buddies: Claire Thoni, Dana Davies-Coffin, and particularly Lynne Foy-Couche. They immediately welcomed me into the fold, supported me, and enabled me to make this book a reality. I will be forever grateful for Lynne's expert suggestions and skilled feedback.

To "Tierney's Team"—uncles Joe and James O'Toole, Sara Nolan, Maria Soriano, Antonieta Hidalgo, Lauren Leon, and Chelsea Wilson. By taking care of the most important job, they gave me the much needed piece of mind to take care of business.

During the long developmental stage of this book, numerous individuals took the time to edit various versions of the text or assist in the advancement of the book in some way: Karen O'Toole, Jennifer O'Toole, Kendel Edmunds, Noreen Franklin, Annie Athon Heck, Chuck Johnstone, Ivette Ricco, Chuck Vedovsky, Connie Hill, Tasha Beaudoin, Nick Clark, Joann Simmons, and Woody Falgoux.

Special thanks for the expertise of Larry Kennan, executive director of the NFLCA, agent Bill Heck, and M. J. Duberstein of the NFLPA's Research Department.

To friends and family who have emotionally supported me during the long journey: Julie Lopez, Kim Schaeffer, Christine Arias, Rocio DeKollo, Lorraine Kumar, Yvonne Lake and Bill Warren, and Laura and Mick Morlan. To my loving parents, Mike and Karen O'Toole; to my siblings, Joe, Jennifer, and James O'Toole; and to Pam and Lyle Sieg. Many thanks are due to my beautiful and special friend Pam. She was always there to answer my "real-quick writing questions" and to lend me a sympathetic ear when things weren't going well. I will never forget her unending support. Thanks to everyone named for offering uplifting words and for encouraging the process of artistic creation!

Last, to the most loyal furry companions a writer could ask for, my dogs Sadie and Frisco.

WEDDED
to the Game

Flowers and First Downs 1

In 1985, when seventeen-year-old Jacqueline Bernice Mitchell met twenty-two-year-old Jerome Lee Rice—who was even then already known by just his first name, Jerry, and who would eventually become perhaps the greatest NFL football player ever—she was a senior in high school and he was a senior college student at Mississippi Valley State. That they met at all was unlikely, and Jackie's first impression of Jerry wasn't exactly love at first sight. But sparks flew from the first moment they laid eyes on each other. Jackie simply calls it fate.

As a Zeta Phi Beta debutante, Jackie and her high school sorority sisters planned a visit to Mississippi Valley State that included a campus tour and tickets to the men's basketball game. Jerry, a Sigma Phi Beta, which is a brother fraternity to the Zetas, also planned to take in the game that night.

However, Jackie came very close to not going at all after she found out the sorority sisters were all told to dress alike in new pairs of jeans. Feeling self-conscious about her older worn denims, Jackie was going to back out. But Jackie's mother, Gloria, said, "Jackie, just go. I'll iron these jeans up for you. I'll put starch in them. I'll make them nice and crisp. They will look just like they are brand new."

Gloria worked her magic, and she and Jackie drove to the school just as the bus was pulling away from the curb. Driving alongside, they honked until the bus stopped and let Jackie aboard.

Not owning the right clothes and doing without were common occurrences in the Mitchell household. With an absentee father and a physically impaired mother, Jackie was far from privileged. When Gloria was eighteen, she suffered a severe stroke that left her partially paralyzed. Only three months later, she became pregnant with Jackie, the family's third daughter. Gloria's physical weakness made the pregnancy very difficult, but almost from the moment Jackie was born, mother and daughter have shared an especially tight bond. Throughout her childhood and teenage years, Jackie helped her mother by becoming, as she says, "like the arm or the leg that she couldn't use."

Jackie learned early on to make the best out of every situation, and she was not the type to let opportunities pass her by. Outgoing and active growing up, Jackie participated in almost every athletic, academic, and community activity available. She was the type of girl who, once she finished her homework, ran outside to play football with the boys or shoot basketballs on dirt courts. When she was only ten, Jackie became the first female to participate in the YMCA-sponsored "Punt, Pass, and Kick Contest," and she just missed making it into the top five. As she grew older, she was smart enough to be listed in the *Who's Who among High School Students* and beautiful enough to win numerous citywide beauty pageants, including Miss Black Greenville Teen in 1984.

Perhaps the most telling incident about Jackie's character, however, concerns her choice of college. As a high school senior, Jackie was awarded a four-year academic scholarship to attend a private liberal arts school in California, but she declined the offer, stating that California was too far away from her mother. Instead, she enrolled at the University of Southern Mississippi as a pre-med student.

Confident, self-possessed, and good-looking—and sporting freshly ironed dark jeans—Jackie stood out among her wide-eyed Zeta sisters at the basketball game that night. The sorority's Sigma college brothers, including Jerry, were quick to take notice of her, but Jackie was not interested. At halftime, her long-time boyfriend was supposed to come pick her up after returning from a different college visit, and he had his own growing reputation as a standout high school quarterback with a national ranking.

An avid college hoops fan, Jackie quickly became annoyed by the distracting commotion in the stands. Before the game had started, and even after, numerous spectators, including many of what she calls "giddy girls," began asking the soon-to-be-drafted Jerry for his autograph. People considered him the best wide receiver to come out of the small Division I-AA Mississippi Valley State. Jerry had amassed an astounding career total of 4,693 receiving yards, and he was turning the heads of NFL scouts from Green Bay to Dallas.

Her concentration on the game already broken, Jackie realized her sports-fanatic uncles would want the rising star's signature, so she soon found her own piece of paper and walked over.

As Jackie recalls the moment in her living room, a relaxed smile warms her face; then she tucks one leg under the other and begins to laugh:

I said, "Excuse me, can I get your autograph?"

He looked at me. I had already checked out all the little responses he had written on the other girls' autographs. It was usually like, "Much success" or "Good luck in the future." You know, things like that.

He asked, "What's your name?" and I said, "Jackie." So, he wrote, "To Jackie: a very beautiful young lady."

I look at it, and I'm like, "I can't take this home to my mom. Can you please write something else?"

Then he wrote on there, "I would like to meet you soon." I thought, "Oh, my God. This guy is hitting on me." So, I ran back to my seat, thinking, "Oh, my God! He's really hitting on me!"

All the girls asked, "What did he write? What did he write?" I said nothing and just folded it up and stuffed it in my pocket.

The game continued, and soon one of Jerry's frat brothers was attempting to get Jackie's attention by passing written messages to her up the bleachers.

She says, "I thought it was very immature. So, I said, 'You know what? If you want to talk to me, come up here and talk. Or, I can come down there. But stop passing notes.' "

Eventually, Jackie was seated next to the frat brother who had been passing the notes, with Jerry on her other side. But when the frat brother began making sexually suggestive remarks, Jackie quickly turned her back on him, so that now she was facing Jerry. Jackie was expecting her boyfriend to arrive at any moment, and while she waited, she and Jerry exchanged some small talk.

Jackie says it didn't take long for the two to get into "this really deep conversation." Taking an immediate liking to her, Jerry fibbed about his age, styling himself as two years younger so that perhaps he might seem less intimidating to the high school senior.

At intermission, Jerry excused himself to visit the concessions stand. Before he left, he asked Jackie if she would like anything to eat or drink. She said no.

Jackie says, "So he goes, and he stays gone for like twenty minutes. Girls are coming out from all over. He'll stop and talk to this girl and then stop and talk to that girl. And I'm just sitting there."

Her boyfriend was still nowhere to be seen, and when Jerry finally returned to his seat, Jackie, both ignored and stood up, was a force to be reckoned with.

"I said, 'Look, that was very rude what you did! I was just left sitting here. Either you can sit here and talk to me, or I can go back to my seat.'

"He said, 'Oh! You're spoiled. You have to have everything your way, huh?'

"I said, 'No, I don't, but just because you're Jerry Rice, don't think you need to have everything your way!' "

They sparred back and forth, "going at each other's throats and everything," Jackie says, even after the second half of the game started. When they eventually settled down, Jerry suggested starting over, and Jackie readily agreed. They exchanged phone numbers, and when the game was over, Jerry attempted to walk her outside, but autograph seekers pulled Jerry in one direction while Jackie's chaperones pushed her in another. Before becoming completely separated, Jerry called out, "Okay, I'll call you tomorrow at noon!" Completely disbelieving that a college football star would ever call a high school senior, Jackie replied, "Okay, okay."

Cupid's arrow must have flown across that hardwood floor with dead aim because at exactly noon the next day Jerry did call Jackie, and three hours after that, he was at her house. When Jackie's mother, Gloria, entered the room to meet him, he promptly stood up to introduce himself and shook her hand, leaving Gloria immediately impressed by the charming young man.

The couple spent the afternoon and evening riding around Greenville's parks in his sports car. By Monday, when he picked her up from school, everyone was already talking about "Jackie and Jerry." Not long after this, Jackie said farewell to her quarterback boyfriend—the one who never showed up at the basketball game to give her a ride home.

At Jerry's invitation, Jackie and her sister were soon traveling to Mississippi Valley State for weekend dances. After the dances, Jerry would hand Jackie the keys to his prized Nissan 300Z. The sisters would jump in the sports car and cruise the campus.

Some female coeds didn't appreciate that a high school senior was now the object of their star athlete's affections. They nicknamed her "the Baby" and began making anonymous, threatening phone calls to her house.

"What do you think he'll want with you?" they would say. "You are just a baby and he's a man. We don't want to see you over here again."

After a trace was put on the phone, Jerry confronted the jealous parties and the calls stopped.

It took a while for Jackie to believe the football star wasn't going to treat her like another female hanger-on, especially with their five-year age difference. His friends and roommates assured her that Jerry did, indeed, find something special about her. They had never seen their friend act this way about a woman. Then one of Jerry's roommates cited perhaps the final proof of his friend's devotion.

"Gosh, he must really like you," the roommate told Jackie, "because *no one* ever drives his car."

When asked what attracted Jerry to her, Jackie replies, "He said I was the most beautiful thing he had ever seen. Then after talking to me, he found out that I was really smart and that I wanted something out of life."

After dating for three years, Jackie and Jerry married on September 8, 1987—and they have been happily married ever since.

A Typical College Romance

Both Jackie and Jerry are uncommon individuals in their own right, and in many ways their marriage is also exceptional, given its strength and longevity in the face of all the stresses that come with such high levels of professional achievement, celebrity, and wealth. However, the story of how they met is actually shared by the overwhelming majority of NFL women I interviewed. With few exceptions, women met their future husbands in college or even high school, and they often married by their early twenties, when the man's football dreams were just that, dreams, and a successful life in the NFL was anything but assured.

Before they met their future NFL husbands, most of these young women were strong-willed and goal-oriented, with high self-esteem, a far cry from the stereotype of the shallow, calculating gold-digger the media sometimes portray. In fact, for many couples, the man's eventual success in the NFL would not have been possible without the emotional and sometimes financial support of his girlfriend or spouse. While the stories of how couples made it to the NFL will be told in the next chapter, the stories of NFL romances serve to illustrate that usually both partners began life together quite young, and neither had any clue if a life in the NFL was possible, nor how long or hard the road to get there would be. In other words, they were no different from college couples everywhere.

Among the women we'll meet in more detail below, Kathryn Lee Karr met her future husband, Mike Waufle, at a high school dance. They went to different schools and had come to the event with other people, but the minute they made eye contact, they began angling for a way to dance with each other.

Kathy says her attraction was simple: "He looked really good. He had a ton of hair and long, long sideburns, which were totally in at the time. I just remember his eyes were beautiful blue. I didn't even know Mike was a football player. He was wearing his letterman's jacket—which said 'Bubba'—but it didn't mean all that much to me."

It was 1970, and Kathy says she was a "hippy dippy"; that night she was wearing "Indian moccasins and bell-bottom tie-dyed jeans." Finally, after hours of circling around each other, Mike approached Kathy. They danced to one fast song, and then it was the last song of the night, a slow one. As the teenagers embraced, Kathy says, "I melted." The couple married about two years later.

Then there is Kimberly Glick. Kim was a standout high school tennis player who had every intention of joining the pro circuit until she broke her leg in an accident after her high school graduation. The gorgeous, blond-haired, 5-foot-9-inch athlete then turned to modeling; she won numerous international bathing suit competitions and even earned bit parts as a movie extra. She was a college student at Notre Dame when she met her future husband, Tim Ruddy, in Notre Dame's bar, The Linebacker. Tim was a center for the Fighting Irish with a genius-level IQ. Kim had dated athletes before, but she says, "I didn't really date athletes that were into brutal sports. Football was less of an attraction for me. The whole limelight I'd already had with tennis. It just wasn't really that exciting for me, that whole aspect of sports."

However, Kim and Tim began dating and eventually married. Kim says matter-of-factly, "It just worked out. We connected real well."

Kori Bevans was a junior at the Massachusetts Institute of Technology, studying mechanical engineering, when she traveled to California for a summer internship and met her future husband, David Shaw. A friend of Kori's took her out to a dance club in Oakland because she thought she needed to meet more people. Kori gave her phone number to several guys that night, but the next day she was waiting for only one call, from David, who had just graduated from Stanford University, where he lettered in football. He did call, and they got together every single day afterward for the rest of the summer of 1995.

"When I met David he had just finished with school, and he was realizing that he wasn't going to play football professionally. He wanted to coach. When he told me he wanted to be a coach, I didn't think anything of it. It was an afterthought. It wasn't until much later on that he told me his dad coached in the NFL and that he also had aspirations to be in the NFL."

Gina Nedney was a cheerleader and her future husband, Joe, was a player for San Jose State's football team. It sounds like the classic football romance, but Gina says, "San Jose State isn't a big school that has a lot of players who go into the draft, so I didn't even think about that. I was attracted to him because he was an environmental major. It helped that I knew him through football and through sports. My parents are huge football fans. I grew up loving football. I think one of the reasons Joe was attracted to me is that I knew all the rules and I love the game."

Kim Courtley met her husband, Mike Singletary—the future Hall of Famer for the Chicago Bears—when she was a freshman and he was a sophomore at Baylor University in Texas in 1978. Mike already had a growing reputation as a football star, but the teenagers were more interested in each other's character.

Kim says, "I was not comfortable at Baylor. All the girls looked like Miss Texas and they were cheerleaders. I was not. I was not even Miss Michigan. I was from Detroit. I just started getting to know some of the football players, and I had a reputation as a girl who was basically not going to have sex with them, which was attractive to Mike. He came from a very religious background, and girls that did that were not attractive to him. He says he knew as soon as he saw me that he was going to marry me. He is that type of person. He is a dreamer. He is a visionary."

Pat Kennan and her husband, Larry, were high school sweethearts who met in biology class, and Pat laughs when she explains her attraction: "Honestly, he was cute. He was interested in me, and I was boy-crazy, and he was a jock."

When I met my future husband, John Morton, I was a sophomore at Western Michigan University. I had been awarded a full university scholarship to play softball for the college team, and I was hoping to escape my tame, rural Michigan upbringing on the strength of my arm and determination. My parents and siblings all excelled in sports, and they strongly supported my softball goals and achievements. However, I knew athletics would carry me only so far—despite the prominence of women's softball at recent Olympic games, a professional league does not exist—so I was also studying sociology and criminology with the intent of becoming a federal criminologist.

The night John and I met began like it does in any number of teenage coming-of-age movies, with several underage teammates and me sneaking into a Kalamazoo bar so that we could dance with older guys. When those same guys, who happened to be members of the football team, showed up outside our apartment later that night, we couldn't have been more mortified. We had already brushed out our hairspray, wiped off our heavy bar makeup, and even passed around white pimple cream.

Under the condition that no lights could be turned on, we let the football players inside for a short visit. Before leaving that night, John asked for my phone number. With the next week filled with final exams, followed by Christmas vacation, I did not expect to hear from him. But I did, and over the course of our first few dates he displayed a romantic, kind, and even gentlemanly side quite atypical for a "jock." This is what convinced me that he was an extraordinary person worth knowing, football player or not.

Rah Rah Sis Boom — Naw

When we met, John was a highly regarded receiver for the Western Michigan University team. In large part because of John's speed, some football analysts thought he might be picked in that April's draft, possibly in a middle round. He wasn't drafted, but he soon signed as a free agent with the Los Angeles Raiders, who asked him to join their training camp that summer.

By that point, John and I had had a wonderful six months together, but when he left for Los Angeles, I told him it was over. In fact, I tried to break up with him several times over the phone while he was there, but he begged me not to. Early on, specifically from the moment I kept his pace while we ran and trained together side by side, John felt we had "a connection." Despite his confidence in our future, I just wasn't sure that I could handle a long-distance relationship with anybody, but especially not one with an NFL player. I knew what the NFL was like, or I thought I did, and John had to work very hard to convince me that not every player spent his off-field time boozing around town and cheating on his girlfriend.

It was only after he asked me to join him in LA for the summer, and I did, that I began to believe we could be serious.

This same trepidation about football players was shared by a number of women I interviewed. Football players have some of the worst reputations among university athletes for the way they treat women, especially in the larger college programs, and the reputation does not get better when they turn professional. Some women, me included, had heard stories in college or even knew of athletes on campus who had sexually, emotionally, and sometimes physically abused women. Rather than making guys more attractive, being a football player was more often a hurdle to romance.

Lori Warhop had known her future husband George for two years before they went on a date, and she'd avoided becoming romantic with him almost solely because he was involved with football. George had played for the University of Cincinnati; when he met Lori, he was an assistant football coach for the University of Kansas. Then, one New Year's Eve, George needed a date to go to a party, so he called Lori's roommate to see if she or Lori were available. Lori's roommate told him, "Oh, I already have plans, but Lori isn't doing anything." This unexpected, unplanned date provided the spark that changed Lori's mind about George.

Lori says, "Football was almost an aversion to me because I had gone to school at the University of Kansas, and I didn't really care for a lot of the football players that I had met there. I thought they were all arrogant. It was a generalization, but to me it didn't matter. It was almost like, 'Oh, you're one of those.' That's why we were just friends for so long."

Kim Ruddy also found Tim's involvement in football to be an obstacle to serious romance at first. "You had a lot of bad things going on in sports at that time, like the whole O. J. Simpson thing. I just didn't want to be part of all the controversy. But then I started to like him as a person, and we both wanted to give each other a chance."

In addition, Kim was concerned Tim might treat her like a groupie. She says, "That is why I didn't like to date football players. Mostly in college that is what you hear and what you see, and I was very concerned by that. I wanted to learn very quickly if he was going to do that or not. Obviously, he didn't."

At the same time, many women to whom I spoke did not express any concerns about getting involved with a football player. This usually had less to do with any neutral or positive image of football players than with a woman's own sense of self and belief in her own judgment. Some women said they simply could sense if someone was a good and decent person or not; being a football player didn't make any difference in their assessment. Nor did these women have concerns about being mistreated—because they wouldn't have put up with it.

Julianne Player, who met her husband in college when he was a punter for the football team, says she never worried about being treated like a groupie: "I don't think I would have let him. I'm not a chaser, so if he thought that I was going to do all the work, he would have been mistaken. And it wouldn't have worked out."

Even Jackie Mitchell turned down Jerry Rice when he first proposed to her. She says, "I have always had dreams and aspirations. I always knew from when I was a kid growing up that I wanted to be a doctor. There are just so many things that I want to accomplish in life, and at that time, it was just not the right decision. I wanted to do a lot of things that I felt marriage would limit me in doing. The dreams and goals for myself, and dreams of helping my family out, my mom, you know.

"At the time of the proposal, Jerry had just gotten drafted, but it was before he actually started playing for the Niners." Laughing, Jackie says simply, "It was too early for me."

Dating a Pro

Significantly fewer women I interviewed began dating their future husbands after their NFL careers had begun. But in their stories as well, the couple's chemistry always had a bigger impact on the future of the romance than the man's employment in professional football.

It also can be true that sometimes NFL men—particularly older, established players—want to make sure that the woman they are dating is in fact falling for them and not for their NFL fame or their presumed wealth. I have heard and have been told that some veteran NFL men will not date a woman unless she is first referred to them by a trusted friend or teammate. Others will put their unknowing dates through "tests."

This was the case for one NFL woman I spoke to. She told me that many years after she and her husband were married, he revealed the truth about their first date. They had been having a great time drinking and dancing at a bar, and he had invited her to have breakfast with him after the bar closed at 2 a.m. She had said no, and her husband told her that if she'd said yes, he would have dumped her. She says, "His opinion of women who would have done that is that it might have been more of a groupie thing than anything real."

Veteran NFL men also seem to be attracted to ambitious, successful women in their own right. Chandra Smith definitely fits this mold. She met her future husband, Dwight Hollier, while they were both students at the University of North Carolina at Chapel Hill. However, they didn't begin dating romantically until after both had graduated; she was about to begin an OB/GYN medical residency in Pittsburgh, and he was a third-year linebacker with the Miami Dolphins.

Growing up, Chandra idolized her family pediatrician, and for as long as she can remember she had insisted that she would be a doctor too. She says, "I have known what I wanted to do since I was seven."

In 1990, Chandra was enrolled in a pre-med summer program at UNC (after graduating from Emory University on a full academic scholarship), and Dwight was a standout senior linebacker on the Tar Heel team who would soon be drafted by the Dolphins. The couple was introduced by mutual friends, and after a group dinner one night Chandra drove Dwight home to his apartment.

Rather than being romantic, Dwight spent the majority of the car ride extolling the virtues of his then girlfriend, even proffering Chandra a photo from his wallet. This didn't bother Chandra, for she had her own love interest at the time, one of Chapel Hill's star basketball players. Still, Chandra recalls being impressed by the thoughtful college senior who spoke in earnest of one day earning his Master's degree in counseling. Unlike some other athletes she had met, Chandra noticed that Dwight did not take on the role of "The Man" and attempt to hit on every woman he met.

She says of their car ride, "I thought, 'That is just so sweet.' He carries his girlfriend's picture, and he is all proud of her."

Over the next three years, Chandra and Dwight saw each other only rarely. During the NFL off season, Dwight made occasional visits to his alma mater, and the pair got together a couple of times, but they never seemed to connect. Once, after meeting at a dance club, Dwight asked Chandra to call him, but she was dating a fellow medical student at the time, and "feeling guilty," she put Dwight's number in her dresser drawer.

Interestingly, the missed opportunities made Dwight more intriguing to Chandra, and she admits to developing "sort of a crush" on him. She began following his career and watching the Dolphins games on television. Returning to Chapel Hill the next year, Dwight left another message for Chandra.

Again they got together, and perhaps the stars had finally aligned because now the duo clicked, and for one whirlwind weekend they found it nearly impossible to part ways. Dwight even postponed his return flight to Miami.

For Dwight, Chandra was refreshing: here was a woman who loved ESPN yet did not dwell on the fact that Dwight played professional football. Chandra was interested in his career, but she was firmly committed to her own as well, and her intellect and independence impressed him. For one thing, she never assumed that he should pay for her meals; she always offered to pay her share. Later on, when the two were dating seriously and Chandra traveled to Florida, she paid for her own plane tickets.

But before the magical weekend had even occurred, Chandra had accepted an OB/GYN residency in Pittsburgh. Ever practical and self-assured, Chandra needed to make sure Dwight was interested in more than a fun fling before things went any further.

She says, "I was not going to put in a request for a particular type of schedule or bend over backwards for a rotation if it wasn't serious. But I told him, 'If you think this relationship is serious, I am willing to put as much effort into it as I need to.'"

Dwight said all the right things, and the couple embarked on that most difficult juggling act, the long-distance relationship. It's one challenge that nearly every NFL couple has to negotiate at some time.

Every nonworking weekend, Chandra spent with Dwight. Some medical rotations were more difficult to schedule around than others, but during the football season, Chandra tried her best to attend all of Dwight's games, whether they were home games in Miami or away games in other cities. Chandra flew to Miami frequently, but she also drove to Cincinnati when the Dolphins played the Bengals, and she flew to Minneapolis when they played the Vikings.

"When I would travel, he would usually break curfew and stay in my room with me," she confides with a laugh. "But when Jimmy Johnson became the head coach, I didn't fly to any away games. I just went to Miami." Chandra says Coach Johnson was known for being extra strict about prohibiting the men from socializing with friends or family on away trips.

Chandra didn't mind the planning, organization, and energy needed to match her and Dwight's busy schedules. She was in love. It was her father who took more convincing that she wasn't making a mistake or wasting her time. Chandra and her father had always been close, and they shared a love of football. But first and foremost, he wanted to protect his daughter.

Chandra says, "When I started dating Dwight and I told my dad he played professionally, my dad said, 'Well, what else can he do?'

"I said, 'Well . . . he has a degree in psychology, and he is planning on getting his Master's.' Dad wanted to know what Dwight was going to do if football didn't work out. He knew that football didn't last long for most people."

Chandra chuckles when remembering these talks. "He wanted to make sure that no one was going to be living off of his doctor daughter."

Chandra's father eventually came around, and after three years of dating, Chandra and Dwight got married. Chandra would go on to complete residencies in internal medicine and general surgery as well, but she eventually decided to specialize in OB/GYN. In part, she decided this because she liked working with women.

She says, "It was a totally different level that we connected on. I felt more comfortable in that field."

In the end, Chandra did not need her father to remind her to stick with her goals. Despite the challenges her two-career marriage entails, she always knew it would be this way.

Of her career, Chandra says, "It was going to be accomplished. It was going to be done. Whomever I ended up with would, number one, understand that, and two, would work with that. If a relationship was meant to be, it was going to last through residency. It was going to make it through a long-distance relationship. We were going to be together when we were meant to be together."

2 In Pursuit of an NFL Dream

The odds of playing or coaching in the NFL are quite slim. According to the National Football League Players' Association (NFLPA), every year approximately 971,000 high school students play organized football. Of these, only 65,000 will go on to play at the college level; only 6,000 will be scouted for the NFL; only 875 will sign NFL contracts; and only 300 will make an NFL roster (and of those, only half will play four or more NFL seasons). In other words, of all the college players in any given year, less than one-half of 1 percent will ever take the field on a Sunday afternoon for an NFL team. In addition, the unofficial rule-of-thumb is that if an NFL player is not a full-time starter within two to four years, he will be a career backup. Likewise, many college coaches work their entire careers without making it to the pros—mainly because the NFL is a small and somewhat guarded circle.

Every year, there are tens of thousands of NFL hopefuls trying to become one of those lucky three hundred. Among those three hundred, the top prospects may make an NFL roster in their first year, but the others will labor two, three, or four or more years trying to break through—during which time they will usually go through a series of training camps, team workouts, and, for some players, even stints in other leagues. Obviously, since no player knows if he will be among the successful ones, many of them keep trying year after year, doggedly believing that they will eventually make it. Except for the athletic prodigies, NFL dreams must be nurtured in the face of extremely discouraging, even overwhelming, odds.

Before they have ever met their football player husbands, most women have already formed their own dreams and goals for the future. I had a promising softball career. Jackie Rice had qualified for pre-med college. Upon falling in love with an NFL hopeful, each woman must, sooner or later, face the practical consequences of her mate's dream on her own life goals. The details differ, but nearly every woman must choose between what she wants to do—academically, professionally, or otherwise—and being with the man she loves.

Whether her husband or boyfriend is still pursuing his NFL dreams or has already achieved them, a woman must usually face the following series of difficult questions: Should I move along with him to each new city, wherever in the country that may be and for however long each stay may last? If that means completely sacrificing my own career, can I live with that? If it means delaying my career, how long can I wait? If it's longer than expected, will that create resentment that destroys our relationship? Then again, if I stay behind to pursue my own goals, will we be able to survive a long-distance relationship? Will we be happy living that way, and how long can *that* last?

Many relationships, especially new ones, cannot survive the pressures that pursuing an NFL life puts on couples. However, those that do survive are particularly strong. In fact, one theory as to why the majority of NFL couples, especially players and their partners, have been together since college and even high school is that their relationships matured more quickly than those of other couples their age. This maturity comes from enduring together from a very early moment the somewhat unique pressures and strains that come with pursuing a life in the NFL.

From the time he is a teenager until his pro career is over, a football player is subject to tremendous demands and expectations. In high school, he has to play his "A" game to become a top college recruit. As a college player, he must put up big stats by his junior year to catch the eye of pro scouts. After he signs with a pro team, it is only *after* he beats out the veterans and makes the starting roster that he can begin to relax. And even then, the pressure to perform on the field (or be replaced) continues for the duration of his pro career.

During the stressful younger years, the player learns to depend on his girlfriend or wife for emotional and sometimes financial support. She becomes his one nonjudgmental constant. When he is with her, he can be himself and not have to play the role of "future NFL star." Having a partner by his side may also make the future seem less intimidating. For the woman, this may in fact be the start of a long series of accommodations and sacrifices she will have to make on her spouse's behalf. For the relationship to work, each partner must display an extraordinary amount of trust, devotion, and faith in each other.

One NFL woman described the following conversation she had with her fiancé, who was then already on an NFL roster: "My husband told me before we got married that my life was going to be totally different. I'd need to just bear with him for the next five to six years, when life would be pretty much about him. If I could just bear with him, afterwards we would be fine because he was going to do his part. I could follow my dreams and do whatever I wanted to do. I have to believe in that."

By the time the man makes it into the NFL, he and his partner have already accumulated a long shared history—some of it good, some of it agonizing, all brought about by his involvement in football. This shared history will serve them well when it comes time to experience, side by side, the trials and tribulations of NFL life itself. Indeed, it will be essential.

Time to Make the Cheese
Kathy and Mike Waufle—whose story of meeting at a high school dance in 1970 was told in chapter 1—married in January 1973. A few months earlier, in the fall of 1972, Mike had enlisted in the U.S. Marines, and for the next three and a half years he was stationed at a base in South Carolina. Ultimately, Mike's life goal was to play defensive tackle in the NFL, and while he was in the military, he kept that dream alive by playing football for the base team.

A few months before his military release, Mike wrote letters of interest to university football coaches throughout the country—he knew that if he had no college experience, the chance that an NFL team would sign him would be slim. However, universities weren't interested in a slightly older armed forces veteran, so Mike changed gears and decided to start at the bottom, with community colleges.

Eventually, Mike was accepted at Bakersfield Community College. At the end of two years, he was a standout defensive lineman who had led his team to a junior college national title and to the 1976 Junior Rose Bowl. With these achievements, the tables turned, and Mike received over a hundred letters from interested four-year colleges. Mike chose Utah State University to showcase his budding NFL potential.

As Mike attended school and felt his NFL dream drawing closer, Kathy worked full-time to support the family; she would have preferred to stay at home with their infant daughter, but, she says, "I went to work because we needed insurance." Kathy got a job packaging cheese at Shriver's Cheese Company on the late-night swing shift. For a year and a half, until she was seven months pregnant with their second daughter, Kathy was the family's sole provider.

"That was tough," Kathy says. "We hardly got to see each other at all. I was working, and he was going to school and had football practice."

And yet Kathy believed that Mike was going to make it to the pros, especially since he'd come this far already. Moreover, as a farmer's daughter from upstate New York, she was no stranger to hard work. She was prepared to do whatever was necessary to support her family until her husband succeeded, even if that meant arriving home every night exhausted and reeking of cheese.

Mike wasn't a superstar at Utah State, but he and Kathy both felt his chances of being chosen in the 1978 draft were decent. When Mike was passed over, they were crushed, but their hopes were reignited after an agent noticed the defensive lineman and offered to represent him. He soon got Mike a tryout with the Dallas Cowboys.

Once she learned about her husband's NFL audition, Kathy thought she would never have to search for another benefits-providing job again. Mike would sign a million-dollar NFL contract, and all their financial worries would disappear. Most important, Kathy would be able to stay at home and raise their two daughters.

After Mike left for his tryout, Kathy held a yard sale. She says, "I just knew that he had signed a huge NFL contract, and we would be wealthy and we would be moving to Dallas. I thought, 'Okay, I want to get rid of this junky stuff,' which I probably bought at a yard sale anyway. So I sold all of our furniture."

After putting Mike through drills and watching him perform numerous physical tests, however, the Cowboys informed him that he was "just a hair too slow to play defense." When a dejected Mike returned home, he was less than thrilled to be eating his dinner from a makeshift cardboard table.

Since Mike was now finished with school, he and Kathy decided to move back to New York State to be closer to family, but the Cowboys' rejection did little to deter Mike's agent. He was soon pushing Mike into another tryout with the Atlanta Falcons. Kathy remembers the agent boldly telling her husband, "If you train very hard and if you listen to me, then I'm going to make you rich."

So Mike trained and trained and trained. He ran the roadways. He lifted weights relentlessly. He did everything in his power to make himself more attractive to NFL teams.

During his training, Mike got a phone call from Bruce Snyder, his former head coach at Utah State. Bruce offered Mike a job as a graduate assistant with the football team. Mike demurred, telling Bruce about his tryout with the Atlanta Falcons in a couple of weeks.

Coach Snyder was frank in his response: "Hey Mike, you're married. You've got two kids now. You've got to start thinking about your life and what's real here." Kathy recalls, "Bruce flat out told him, 'I don't think you are good enough. Anyways, this is the real thing.' That was hard for Mike."

But the farmer's daughter was practical, and the NFL had just taught them a harsh lesson: until the cash is in the bank, don't dump the old sofa. Kathy knew that in football as in life, the name of the game is as much *who* you know as *what* you know, and she could sense that Bruce Snyder was an up-and-coming coach. If Mike decided to pursue this opportunity, it would benefit his coaching career to be associated with Snyder. And she was proved right, for Coach Snyder would become one of the nation's first highly paid college coaches.

Despite the continuing financial challenges it would entail—in the late 1970s, Mike stood to earn little more than $2,000 a year as a graduate assistant—Kathy supported her husband as he accepted the offer. This then became Mike's NFL dream: if he couldn't get to the pros on his physical abilities, then he would make it using his mind. But someday, Mike told his young wife, he was going to be an NFL coach.

Again, Mike had to start at the bottom. Kathy, meanwhile, had to find another full-time, benefits-paying job that she could juggle with two kids. To keep their living expenses minimal, the family moved into the Utah State football dorm. In exchange for free rent, she and Mike were responsible for supervising players, conducting room inspections, and managing the dorm facilities. Looking back, Kathy laughs at a particular evening duty: "I had to lock the doors every night after a certain time, trying to keep the maniac girls out."

It took eighteen years—almost two decades—of coaching up the college divisional ladder and building a reputation before Mike finally landed his first NFL coaching job in 1997; it was with the Oakland Raiders.

Kathy says, "Being a farmer's daughter really prepared me for what I had to do. I helped my family work really hard on our farm and the land. I grew up with a lot of ups and down, as I have throughout my career as a football wife. I think that makes you stronger. Over the years you see a lot of things happen to other people that are a whole lot worse than what we have gone through. So no matter how bad it gets, it can always get worse. You've got to count your blessings."

Kicked Around

On the road to the NFL, detours and rough beginnings are common. My husband John spent five years trying to make it into the NFL as a wide receiver: two years were spent on practice squads, two were spent in the Canadian Football League and the World League (or NFL Europe), and there were numerous failed training camps in between. (The NFL World League is similar to professional baseball's farm league; it's the place NFL teams send players to improve their skills.) Like Mike Waufle, John eventually reached the league as a coach, and since then he has been fortunate enough to gain a relative measure of security. Until that point, however, I worked as a bartender, a campus security officer, and a nursing home activities director. Kathy Waufle's story and mine are not unique. If not for their spouses' unwavering belief and support, many men would have been forced to shelve their NFL dreams before they were realized in order to find a better paying, more stable job in some other field.

No matter how much they thought they were prepared, most women I interviewed acknowledged they could never have anticipated the difficult and sometimes unpleasant surprises that awaited them. In my case, it was horribly upsetting to be sitting in a hotel room, desperately thinking of ways I could console my boyfriend when he was cut after only five weeks of Raiders camp. It's one thing to know that your husband's career in the NFL, if he makes it, is likely to last half as long as the time it took to get there, and it's another to live it.

Lori Warhop, whose husband, George, is a coach, says,

"I've had to move and be adaptable to new things and learn how to do things by myself. I'm alone a lot."

In some ways, the journey to the NFL is similar to what couples go through when one partner is in law or medical school. Owing in large part to the steady support of one's spouse, the person is allowed to focus almost entirely on graduating into his or her chosen profession. The difference is that once a person is done with law or medical school, he or she will always have a professional title and the status it confers. For NFL hopefuls, there is no diploma just for learning, and with each passing year, a player's chances of graduating diminish ever more sharply.

One player's wife described her husband's journey this way: "He didn't end up getting drafted [out of college] because of his shoulder. We went on for the next two years with rehab. He was actually picked up as a free agent. He went to the Saints and was released. Came back and went to the World League and was released. Came back and went to the Broncos and was released. Came back and went to the World League and finally made it and did great. It was a bumpy road. You sit by the phone and wonder, Are they going to call? How long is he going to be there?"

Although Scott Player's five-year journey to the NFL has been characterized by the media as a football "Cinderella story"—à la league MVP and rags-to-riches quarterback Kurt Warner—it is actually more typical than people realize. Scott and his wife, Julianne, met when both were attending Florida State University (FSU). Scott originally attended FSU on a baseball scholarship, but he tore his rotator cuff. Realizing his baseball career was finished, he switched his focus to punting. Walking on and winning the starting job on FSU's football team left him with only one year of eligibility—not a lot of time to attract the attention of the pros.

After graduation, the couple lived near the University of Florida in Gainesville, where Julianne worked for Delta Airlines at the airport. Julianne's ultimate goal was to become a television news anchor, and she had every intention of pursuing that goal while Scott pursued his dream. But her job with Delta had an unexpected perk: every time an NFL scout flew in to check out a Florida player, she would call Scott to tell him. He would then rush to the university and hang out, waiting for the opportunity to meet the scout, introduce himself, and try to convince the person to watch him punt.

Julianne recalls, "He would tell the scouts he had played at FSU, and some of them wouldn't believe him. Most wouldn't give him the time of day. I can imagine the first thing teams would think was that this guy wasn't even good enough to get an agent."

In 1995, Scott got a job booming balls for the Birmingham Barracudas in the Canadian Football League, so he and Julianne moved to Birmingham, Alabama. This worked out well for Julianne, as she subsequently got a job at the local television station in the traffic department, providing instruction for the on-air programmers. She also did commercial voice-overs for local businesses and soon felt her own career beginning to grow.

Unfortunately, the Birmingham Barracudas folded after one season. Then, in 1996, at age twenty-six, Scott attended his first NFL camp with the Arizona Cardinals, but they cut him before the regular season began. That year, he received subsequent tryouts with Miami, St. Louis, Washington, Tampa Bay, and the New York Jets.

Dejected, Scott sat out of football for a year while Julianne worked, and the couple decided to get married. Then, in 1997, Scott signed another NFL contract with the New York Giants, who instead allocated Scott to their team in the NFL World League: the Frankfurt Galaxy in Germany.

While Scott went to Germany, Julianne stayed in Birmingham, working at the television station. She says, "Of course, I was sad that we would be apart for so long, but I thought it would be a wonderful life experience for him, and it was a step in the right direction for football. I just wished I could have been there to share it with him, but my job was our only source of steady income and insurance."

For Scott, it was a long and lonely four months of eating bland hotel food day after day and not speaking the native tongue. Scott would ride the team bus back to the Holiday Inn, lie on his double bed, stare at the blank walls, and try not to think about the wide blue ocean that stood between him and his new wife.

The couple's sacrifice went unrewarded when the Giants drafted a punter and cut Scott at the end of training camp. Watching yet another NFL season pass Scott by, the couple decided it was time to move on. They were ready for a home and more stability. To that end, Scott got a job working fourteen-hour days as a dispatcher with a trucking company, and their household was finally bringing in two fixed paychecks. The dispatcher job didn't last long.

After several months, the Cardinals tracked him down again. Their punter had become a free agent, and they told Scott that if he came to camp, he would have a fair chance to win the job. The "fair chance" proclamation had a measure of believability because it came from the Special Teams coach, Al Everest, who had also been Scott's Special Teams coach in the Canadian Football League. Although the couple trusted Coach Everest, there was still some hesitation.

Julianne remembers the defining moment. "We went back and forth, but there was really no decision to be made. As long as there was an opportunity to play, he had to take it."

Such a day eventually arrives for all "journeymen" couples. John and I faced the same dilemma after his own five years of trying. Should he continue getting kicked around, mentally and physically abused by teams in his pursuit to keep his NFL dream alive? Or was it time to get out, accept life without football, and make peace with the fact that he had never "made it"? The emotional upheaval we experienced every time he signed and then was released from a contract was definitely starting to strain our relationship. Yet I knew better than to advise John on whether he should keep trying. Years later, I didn't want to be blamed for John not giving his dream "one last shot."

One player's wife described getting to this moment and the difficulties of remaining supportive. She says her husband was signed as a free agent to an NFL team, but "it lasted like two days. He failed his physical and came home. He went back to Europe, failed his physical, and came back home. He called me first. It's hard because you can't be angry with him. You're obviously angry because of the situation, but it's out of your control. What can we do? We really have to evaluate, How long are we going to do this? How long are we going to try? Because he was out three years and barely getting chances to have a workout, let alone have a job. It is a mental battle. I tried not to blame him. You can blame someone if they don't try, but how can you blame someone if they try?"

There is no easy answer; it's a moment of decision that some reach sooner than others and to which some couples return several times. Player agent Bill Heck, who has represented and counseled many young NFL hopefuls, puts it as follows:

> If a player has been with three or four teams for training camp and hasn't stuck with a team, then maybe I will advise him to move on to life after football. If I feel that I cannot help the player any more—or if numerous teams have told me that it is time for him to move on—then I will tell him so. Some guys recognize this and move on, but some do not have anything else to do and try lower levels of professional football. The guys that have significant others have to actually make a decision. For example, you might have a professional wife, and how long can she put this on hold and still be supportive? This is a point you come to as you get older and as you get tired.

Injuries often precipitate a crisis of commitment, even once you make it in the NFL. I spoke to one player's wife whose husband was cut by his team after an injury and who was trying to work his way back to the NFL. For her, the crisis inspired a renewed determination. She says, "That was really hard. It was just an entire year of chaos. I was almost glad that it happened because my family and my friends really were able to see the real me—how I had to kick in and take over—and see what we really go through. That was almost like, you know what, I was meant to do this. I'm very good at it. I'm a great mom and I'm [Steven's] wife, and if we get back in the NFL, I really think that this past year has helped me to change my view. I would change the way I do things. I'm in it for the long haul with him, and he is with me."

Julianne and Scott Player obviously made the right decision. In 1998, at age 28, Scott finally made an NFL roster—with the Arizona Cardinals, the first team to ever cut him.

Julianne speaks for many NFL women when she says, "I don't think you ever take anything for granted, especially after the long road that he had. When he was in camp in '98 with the Cardinals, they cut the other punter after a couple of weeks of training camp, and Scott was the only one left. No one ever came up to him and said, 'It's your job, and we're not bringing anybody else in.' We were in denial the first few weeks until camp was over. I wasn't going to quit my job to move there until the final roster came out and his name was on it."

Two years later Scott was selected to the NFC Pro Bowl team, and he still punts today for the Cardinals. With heart-touching sincerity, Julianne asserts, "He never gave up. He never stopped practicing. He is the most disciplined person I know. He has worked hard and truly appreciates the privilege of playing in the NFL."

A Year in the Life **3**

In 1998, my husband John got his first job as an offensive assistant coach for the Oakland Raiders (he went on to become the assistant wide receiver coach and then the tight-end coach), and in July 1999, we got married. Prior to the wedding, the other coaches' wives threw me a bridal shower, during which I opened many very pretty and delightful gifts, including an exquisitely wrapped dual set of orange-handled . . . screwdrivers. The look of confusion and surprise on my face must have been evident because the gift giver slowly explained that one tool was called a "Phillips" and the other a "flathead."

"Welcome to the world of coaches' wives, Shannon," she deadpanned. "Do yourself a favor and learn how to use them. Johnny surely won't be around to do things for you."

Wrapping my right hand around the foreign steel objects, I chuckled. Four years and one door frame, half a dozen wall-anchored drapery rods, and two six-foot built-in attic shelves later, I am no longer laughing. In hindsight, I should have opened a wedding gift registry at Home Depot. Though the screwdrivers were a practical gift in years past, I can unequivocally state that electric, cordless, 14.4-volt drivers, with accompanying drill bits, are the only way to go.

By marrying an NFL coach, I actually married two men. The man I fell in love with I call "Off-season John." Energetic, attentive, and easy to be with, he and I have a lot of fun together. We cuddle in front of the TV, go out to dinner with friends, take the baby and our dogs for walks by the lake, and sometimes bring along our mountain bikes and cycle along the rocky shoreline. We joke and laugh and have the greatest of times—that is, from February to mid-July.

"In-season John" is another man entirely. In fact, I hardly ever see him, and when I do, he is perpetually exhausted, either having arrived home from a sixteen-hour day or rushing out the door to begin another one. There is no cuddling on the couch, no dinners out. For him, there is nothing but work, and then more work, and then a little more work besides, in a daily cycle that is only broken by three or fours hours of sleep. When he is not asleep, his only concern—aside from making sure his wife and daughter are still breathing—is to win the next football game. Not even Christmas keeps him home. After a few hours of opening presents and good cheer, he is in his car and pulling out of the driveway. From mid-July to January, this is the man I married.

This same schizophrenic existence is lived by every NFL couple or family. And it takes some getting used to. Some women, particularly coaches' wives, never get over the difficulties and loneliness the football season brings, and as years pass they become increasingly bitter and hostile. Most couples must, at the very least, go through a "transition period" between the in- and off-seasons, during which they find a new balance they can live with. Typically, the longer women are in the league, the better they are able to handle, emotionally and logistically, these transitions, as well as the high toll the game exacts from their husbands or boyfriends. Generally speaking, coaches' wives must learn to cope with the season's endless long hours, and players' wives must learn to deal with their partners' physical pain and injuries, which can be tremendous.

Since the in-season lives of players and coaches can be vastly different from their off-season lives, they are described separately in this chapter. This is followed by a description of the one thing that everyone in the NFL agrees makes it all worthwhile: the playoffs and a trip to the Super Bowl. Then we'll look at that awkward, mostly blessed time, the off-season.

Are You a "Grinder"?

In today's high-stakes NFL, there are hundreds of professional coaches, and there are many in colleges as well, that fit John's mold. During the season, NFL head coaches and their assistants can easily put in upwards of eighty to one hundred hours per week, every week, for about six months. Those who can do this become what is known in football circles as "grinders"; being called a grinder is in its own way the highest compliment a coach can receive. It refers to a breed of men who can sit every day in darkened offices breaking down game film and formulating new plays until their foggy, sleep-deprived brains finally exhaust and sputter like a doused flame.

One coach's wife described how she used to react early in her husband's career: "When I got mad at my husband, I would say, 'You know what, it really takes a special person to sit in the dark with a clicker and watch people run backwards all day.' It would just burn him. Isn't it just stupid, though? Half of their life is sitting in the dark."

Typically, every team has about fifteen to twenty coaches on staff. There is the head coach, the offensive and defensive coordinators, and then about six assistant position coaches on both offense and defense. Below them are lower-level assistants and the offensive and defensive quality-control coaches, who do a lot of the grunt work.

Despite the extreme dedication that all the coaches on NFL coaching staffs bring to their jobs, not all are paid the same, nor do they receive the same recognition. The same is true for players, and this in itself isn't surprising. Head coaches and the offensive and defensive coordinators shoulder the most responsibility for their team's performance, and they get paid the most by a wide margin (salaries will be discussed in more detail in chapter 8). On the other hand, assistant position coaches, who make up the bulk of coaching staffs, earn only a fraction as much, despite often working just as hard, and their efforts are usually underappreciated and overlooked by the media and fans—that is, until their players screw up on the field, and then the coaches get fired.

Larry Kennan, a retired coach and currently the executive director of the National Football League Coaches' Association (NFLCA), believes that NFL owners use these assistant coaches' love of the game against them. First organized in 1983 and officially established in 1996 as a nonprofit labor organization, the NFLCA is the coaches' trade association, and today it is comprised of over seven hundred members. The NFLCA advocates on behalf of coaches for better pay, uniform and dependable medical benefits, better working conditions, and other issues. However, unlike the players' association, the NFLCA does not have a strong bargaining position because it is not a union. Players can strike successfully if they feel they need to, and they have, but coaches cannot, and perhaps it wouldn't be effective if they did because college coaches could come in to fill their shoes.

While coaches have gained some league-wide improvements in benefits such as salary increases through the efforts of the NFLCA, they remain largely at the mercy of their individual teams in terms of their day-to-day working conditions. For instance, during the work week, when coaches "hit the wall," some are able to find their way to their cars and drive home. Others don't make it out of their chairs and fall asleep at, or under, their desks. Out of "consideration" for these dedicated men, many teams have added "bedrooms" to their facilities. These tend to be makeshift storage areas that have been fitted with cots or a couple of twin beds adorned with semi-clean comforters and pillows—not exactly the sort of NFL "perk" most folks imagine.

During the season, with only minor variations among teams, the only time off coaches enjoy is possibly one, or very rarely two, days during the Bye Week (which refers to the one week each season when the team doesn't play), the Friday evening before a home game, and the evening following a game.

The coaching staff's schedule for the week is set by the head coach, but it typically starts first thing Monday morning with a critique of the previous Sunday's game with the offensive and defensive coaching staffs and then again with the players. This is followed by a brief walk-through on the field to correct any errors in the game that may have occurred.

Tuesdays are coaches' killer nights. The game plan, painstakingly tailored for the upcoming opponent the previous day, has to be implemented, and by Wednesday morning, it needs to be copied and distributed to the players. Thursday and Friday are taken up with morning meetings and afternoon practice, followed by late-evening meetings. Saturday consists of morning meetings and a walk-through. Some of the coaches are then free to leave in the mid-afternoon, but they must return for evening meetings. And Sunday is when they find out if the week's efforts were worthwhile.

Instead of working until midnight every night, some coaches, like my husband, prefer to set their alarms "early," as in 3 a.m., so they can come home "early," as in 9 or 9:30 p.m. John does this so that he might spend thirty minutes or so with his daughter in the evening, and it is not uncommon for coaches' wives to let their children stay up way past a "normal" bedtime just so they can get a glimpse of their fathers.

Over the years, I've realized that I no longer need to consult game schedules. I can inspect John's eyelids when he arrives home to find out how many games remain in the season. When most of the whites of his eyes are visible, it is early in the season, around August or September. When the lids are halfway closed, it's midseason, October through November. And when John's eyelids require toothpicks to stay propped open, it's usually December, and the season, blessedly, is almost finished.

Drive-by Husbands

It was on one of those demanding Tuesday nights that one coach's wife (whom I'll call Karen) phoned her husband to say she needed to go to the hospital. Karen was several months pregnant and had become violently sick to her stomach, so her obstetrician had told her to check into the hospital immediately for intravenous fluids.

After listening to Karen explain what was happening, her husband asked, "So how are you going to get there?"

Though she had spent only a few years in the NFL, Karen was prepared for this response, and she told him she'd already arranged for a girlfriend to drive her. Of her friend, Karen says, "She helped me to my room and got me situated; then referring to my husband's bringing me home, she asked, 'So, Karen, when he picks you up, is he going to honk or come in?'"

Karen understands how this story makes her husband look, but she also understands, and understood then, the intense pressure under which coaches work. Particularly new coaches, as her husband was then, feel that their jobs are at stake almost every week.

Karen says, "I was pregnant with our third, and that was putting pressure on him to provide. He wouldn't verbalize it, but I know that is how he felt. Asking me how I was going to get to the hospital was insensitive, but his intent was not to be rude."

This story perfectly illustrates the lengths to which lack of power and lack of control drive assistant NFL coaches. They feel that taking personal time to focus on something other than winning the next football game — even if it is just for a couple of hours — could leave a black mark next to their names. Their fear is omnipresent: owners, administration, and even other coaches might think, "Aw, we don't want him. He's not a grinder."

One veteran coach's wife agreed that coaches are driven by this mentality, but she thought that necessity wasn't always the root of it. She says, "I think most of it is ego-driven. It is just that mentality of so-and-so works sixteen hours. If I work eighteen, then I am that much better."

Nevertheless, in their responses to my anonymous survey, a number of coaches' wives made supportive remarks similar to Karen's. Some were clearly fed up over complaints by other wives about coaches' long hours. Some wrote comments like, "Wives need to stop complaining and just be thankful their husbands love their jobs" and "I have always taken care of all things at home and put my husband's career as the number 1 priority."

Indeed, it was the opinion of many wives, whether or not they knew initially what they were getting into by marrying a coach, that they eventually needed to make peace with their situation in order to feel happy and satisfied with their lives. One coach's wife I interviewed put this well, saying the following:

I don't count on him for things that I know I can handle. For example, I'll talk to a wife, and she will say, "I am so mad. I have a flat tire, and my husband can't come and get me." And I am thinking, "Call AAA." I mean, that is what I have always done. It never occurred to me that my husband would come and fix the tire.

The women that I have found that are unhappy are the ones

whose expectations are never met. Their expectation is that their husbands are going to get to go to the fall sports banquet and then afterwards they are going to come home and put a new light bulb in. When they don't do it, the wives are constantly mad at their husbands, constantly.

She concludes: "It is what it is. You have a choice: you can either be resentful or deal with it. A lot of wives choose to go with the unhappy and miserable side. It just doesn't change anything, and it won't make you happy."

But being understanding of a husband's work commitments doesn't necessarily make the challenge of being alone and having to fend for oneself easier. One woman wrote, "Until people get to know you, they have no idea how much you have to do on your own, because they have no idea how all-encompassing coaches' jobs are. I am always compared to a single mom."

Another coach's wife says, "When we first got together, I would get home, and I would wait and wait for him to be home. It was like I was always waiting for something. When he got home, I would be like: Good, you're home, now play with me. Because he is so understanding, it didn't reflect badly on our relationship, but if it were somebody else, I could see him being annoyed and be like: Back off, leave me alone. Now, though, I make sure I have a lot going on, so I don't need him to entertain me."

Several women said that friends have no idea what their lives as a coach's spouse are like. One woman said, "I have got really, really good friends that my husband has never met. There are people in our neighborhood that will walk by and wave, and he doesn't know who they are. He'll look at me and say, 'Who is that?' People don't get it, in essence. They don't get it that he leaves before I even bat an eye in the morning and that I'm back in bed way before he gets home. That's hard. And they don't believe it's hard."

Another coach's wife described one way she copes with her "mystery husband": "When we moved into a new neighborhood and the buzz started—'The coach has moved in'—I would have in the off-season a coffee or an open house and invite the neighbors to meet my husband. I said to him that I thought these people thought my husband was a figment of my imagination. I didn't think they believed that I had a husband. They had never seen one. They see me, they see the kids, they see two cars—then one car is missing, but they never saw who drove it away. That way everybody would get to chit-chat with him at least once . . . in the three years we lived there before we were gone!"

As with any challenge, meeting it can strengthen a relationship. This is what Kathy Nolan, whose husband Mike was the defensive coordinator for the Baltimore Ravens at the time of our interview, described happening in her marriage: "NFL women need to learn to verbalize, whether in an argumentative way or in another way, to get their point across. Otherwise, there is so much passive-aggressiveness that goes on; they are just angry in a quiet way. [Mike and I] both had to learn how to communicate better. Part of the way we learned was by going through difficult times. Being alone and not near family—and not being able to depend on anyone but each other—we had to learn how to communicate and lean on each other. I was grateful for that. If I had lived closer to my family, I would have turned to someone other than him, and he to someone other than me."

Nevertheless, despite their efforts not to, some coaches' wives start to resent the demands their partners' jobs put on them and their families. They become disenchanted with "NFL life," no longer happy being Super Moms and self-sacrificing wives. On her survey, one woman wrote: "All coaches wives seem to be very strong and confident, but the veteran wives seem to be a little hard, negative, and detached."

One veteran coach's wife says, "From the amount of women I have known in the NFL, it doesn't appear that the men have as many issues. The women have more envy and a lot more anger and resentment. The resentment is sometimes targeted toward their husbands for making them move around. There is a lot of anger; [for example] they might hate where they are because it snows. Those women are everywhere. There is always someone who just hates where she lives. Then there are those that feel very angry that their husbands are not the coordinators. So they have envy, and they will make some nasty remarks."

At the other extreme are women who buy into "the-game-is-first-at-all-costs" mentality, which is the motto of some coaches.

For instance, when the adult daughter of a coach's wife confessed to her that she had been raped two years earlier, the wife withheld the information from her husband—the girl's father—for a week, since she felt it would be "better for his focus" if she told him after game day Sunday.

Other women said that in essence they did the same thing all the time; they are constantly evaluating what information is important enough to share with their husbands. One wife says, "If there is something going on with our families that can wait, I wait because I don't know how that is going to affect him. I try to block out everything. If there is someone asking him for money, or if someone is sick, or if there is something that I feel that he really has no control over, then I might just wait until afterwards."

Coaches' wives can become desperately lonely during the season. Like many women with absentee partners, they often use their children to fill the void. Regarding having babies, one long-time NFL woman likes to say: "What else is there to do when you are a coach's wife?"

When asked what the biggest challenges were for NFL women, coach's wife Kathy Nolan responded thoughtfully:

Fitting in and finding your place. I'm sure people would say that the guys are never home. I am used to that by now. I mean there are a lot of jobs nowadays where the dads or moms aren't home. It certainly doesn't make things easier as a family that he isn't home so much. It would be interesting to interview somebody now, ten years ago, and in the future. Women would change their answer about what is difficult. Now, I have high-school-aged kids, so moving is the biggest thing. When the kids were little, he was never here. It was the challenge of being home alone and feeling like a single parent sometimes. I've thought, when the kids are gone, will I be as cool with his hours?

Last but not least, coaches' wives are concerned with the state of their husbands' health, which is compromised by their high-stress occupation. Although coaches have state-of-the-art exercise equipment at their fingertips, few have the time or the energy to use it, nor is the teams' catered food known for being particularly healthy. Only recently have some coaches made the link between their lack of exercise and poor diet to several serious medical conditions that are endemic to the coaching ranks, such as weight gain, elevated blood pressure, and high cholesterol.

About NFL coaches' health issues, NFLCA executive director Larry Kennan says, "I don't have any stats, but I have a very strong opinion about it. Coaches die from two things: cancer and heart problems. I believe the heart and cancer problems are the direct result of stress and overwork. Most coaches are former athletes, so they may be in a little better condition than the average guy on the street, but it is a hard life."

Though his evidence is anecdotal, Kennan cites a startling number of coaches who have died in recent years of cancer or heart disease, and these coaches were relatively young, either in their mid-fifties or early sixties. Besides becoming fearful of impending widowhood, wives are very frustrated by dismal statistics like these. Their husbands do not have the same rights and protections as players. If an NFL coach complains about the hours or otherwise expresses his displeasure with his situation, he will be quickly replaced by the throngs of ever-so-willing lower-level coaches.

Despite these health concerns, NFL wives don't want their husbands to leave a job that they love. Not everyone gets to say that about their work. As one coach's wife wryly put it, "He says he was born to coach. What am I supposed to do—tell him he can't?"

Playing for a Living

If not for the protection of the NFLPA, players probably would be forced to hand over their hearts, souls, and their kids' Saturday soccer matches to the NFL, not just during the season, but year round as well. Established in 1956, the NFLPA is a strong union that monitors the terms of the league's collective bargaining agreement, which regulates every aspect of what the NFL can and cannot require of players. The NFLPA represents players for all issues concerning wages, benefits, working conditions, and any other rights. In 1982 and 1987, the association demonstrated its muscle when the players went on strike.

The NFLPA is one reason the lives of players and coaches are so different. Another reason is the nature of their work. Coaches can analyze and draft plays for twelve hours at a stretch, and the worst that might happen is eyestrain and neck ache. But workouts and daily practices for a player are tremendously draining and can be only slightly less hazardous than game day itself. Players work far fewer hours than coaches, but many wives say they pay a far higher price with their bodies, and this alone warrants their higher status and paychecks.

During the season, players typically follow the same set routine week after week. On Monday they come in mid-morning and lift weights. Then they watch film and go over mistakes from the previous game with their position coaches. Tuesday is an official day off for all the players in the league. Healthy players get to spend that day any way they want, and they typically like to be with their families, relaxing at the movie theatres or doing charitable work. But if athletes are in need of medical treatment or rehabilitation, they are required to come in on Tuesday—and to arrive early and/or stay late on most other days. A handful of players will come in and watch film on their day off or work on extra things. On Wednesdays and Thursdays athletes put in their longest days, usually eight hours, which includes running and weight lifting, morning meetings, and a walk-through of plays. There is another meeting after lunch, then the team practice. These days are over around 4:30 or 5 p.m. Fridays and Saturdays are "short" days of three to five hours in which players prepare for the upcoming game by again walking through the plays they are going to be running on Sunday.

In general, this schedule leaves players with much more time at home during the season than coaches could ever dream of having, and perhaps as a consequence, players' wives spoke more enthusiastically about their lives during the season.

Kim Ruddy, whose husband Tim is a starting center for the Miami Dolphins, says, "I love my in-season lifestyle. I have my husband home every night at 6:30 p.m. at the latest, and we have a nice family dinner. Of course, he is gone all day, but in the world people are gone all day. It's a hard adjustment from May to August, when they're off in camp and you don't see them for weeks on end. Normal in-season is nice. We seem to have more of a routine. I've got kids. I live on a routine. It's more settling for me."

Where coaches' wives speak of looking forward to the one night a week their husbands might be home, players' wives sometimes look forward to the few nights their husbands are away. One woman says, "Our in-season lifestyle is so much more structured. We get up. We know he's going to be gone. We do our thing. He comes home. We eat dinner, and the kids go to bed. During the season he's home all day on Tuesdays, and that's when we'll do family things. He's gone on weekends. I almost like having one night a week to myself. It's kind of nice. You can clean the house. You can just count on that time to do what you need to do."

This uninterrupted routine can have its drawbacks. Listening to their coach continually harp on technique, smelling the same stale locker room, and running the same plays over and over—the daily repetitiveness of practice—can wear down even the most driven guys. Monotony is something that all players and teams must work through. NFL athletes also need to be tough mentally to withstand the continual pressure to perform.

Coping with stress over results on the field was another issue mentioned by players' wives, such as the following: "In-season is very busy. My husband is gone all the time, and when he comes home he is very, very tired. It's so emotional during the season. . . . There is more at stake. I'm less demanding of him and his time. I'm kind of his buffer to people."

By far the most stressful issue facing players and their spouses during the season is physical injuries. Everything that is written about the repeated, horrendous abuse that football players endure—particularly high-impact positions like linebacker and running back—is true. Every player spends a portion of his week tending to deep-tissue bruises; hard, painful goose eggs; and skin lacerations—and these wounds are considered simple annoyances. Gridiron stars also typically play through bone, tendon, and ligament damage. Why? The unspoken message NFL players receive is clear: if they are not on the field doing their job, someone else will be. So they shut up, suck it up, and find a way to play through it, despite the pain.

When the player in question is the person you love, passively watching as his worn, battered body succumbs to repeated brutality every week can be agonizing. It would be surprising if spouses didn't feel strongly. Some of the comments they wrote included the following: "They cannot be paid enough in exchange for the long-term effects of injuries." "For what they go through physically, as well as what the owner makes off them, many are underpaid. Baseball and basketball players get guaranteed contracts; NFL players do not."

One wife went so far as to say, "The NFL is glorified slavery in some respects."

One offensive lineman's girlfriend told me that during the season, she launders the couple's bedsheets every day. At night her boyfriend's scabbed-over elbows crack, oozing blood and puss on the bedding. Recalling his first season, she says, "I remember he took his shirt off, and he was covered with bruises, scrapes, and bumps. I was on the verge of tears, and I asked him, 'Are you sure this is what you want to do? You have a college education. You can do whatever you want. Is this what you want?' He said, 'Yes, this is it.' So we just go with it."

Wives and girlfriends of players must all at some time become nurses for their men. Kim Ruddy has seen her husband injured numerous times and undergo several surgeries. She says, "I try to be there with whatever he needs. I'm kind of everybody when he is hurt. I kind of take over all roles—mother, father, grandparents, and nurse. He is a guy, and guys don't like to stay in bed, but I try to be there for him and help him as much as I can, even if it's just putting the ice pack on the shoulder or helping him get the sling back on. In our home, we definitely play as a team."

Nevertheless, injuries are a fact of life in the NFL, and players, if not their wives, typically downplay them. As one woman says: "Oftentimes, he will be hurt, and he won't tell me. He handles pain very well. Last year he played with a broken wrist. He is matter-of-fact about injury. If he is in pain, he doesn't mention it."

The following story by Julianne Player is typical of the dilemma over injuries that many, if not all, athletes must face. Scott Player had just signed as a punter with the Arizona Cardinals—his first job in the NFL after five years of trying (that story is told in chapter 2). Julianne says:

We had just moved to Arizona. I had just quit my job. We

were living in a hotel, and the day that he came home with a pulled calf [muscle] was the day we were supposed to sign for our house. So that was kind of stressful. He had only played a couple of weeks into the season, and we didn't know if he was going to have a job the next week. Players sign contracts, and Scott signed for three years, but the contract is one-sided. The team can cut you at any point.

So when he came home injured, my fear was that we had just moved out to Arizona and, heaven forbid, this injury would cost him his job. It was his one big break, his shot at the NFL. The injury happened on a Thursday afternoon, and Friday morning they had two other punters and were working them out. That is a reality check. They had to carry Scott off the field; that is how bad he pulled his calf. It was the last run of practice, and it threw the whole place into a panic.

Friday morning, they gave Scott a choice. They knew he was hurt, and he could punt knowing that he wasn't going to do well, or he could rest his leg and let somebody else punt for a week or two, and then he could take over when he got better. But the risk is that the other guy is going to get in, have two good games, and then they're not going to want you back. Scott had worked so hard to get to where he was that he didn't want anyone else to take his position. He didn't want anybody else to have a chance to come in and do well. They gave him the option, and he took the option to play injured.

Take Me to "The Dance"

As frantic as I often am for the end of the season, as much as I want John to be home *now*, if there is a chance for our team to make it to "The Dance," "The Show," or "The World Championship"—to get, that is, into the playoffs and to the Super Bowl—I wouldn't mind in the least for the season to be prolonged. No matter how tired and ready for a break everyone is at the end of the regular season, when your team is on a championship run, it's like hot blood racing through nearly collapsed veins.

It doesn't matter if you've never been before or if it's your second or third trip. It doesn't matter if you're a twenty-one-year-old impressionable girlfriend or a fifty-five-year-old jaded NFL wife; a novice mom with an infant or an expert with several teenagers; a career-oriented businesswoman or a domestic goddess: there ain't no NFL woman immune to Super Bowl fever.

Pat Kennan—whose husband Larry Kennan is now executive director of the NFLCA but who started his first professional coaching job with the Raiders—feels that winning in the playoffs made a difference in their lives "big time." She says, "It's the self-fulfillment, and you feel you have some job security. I think those two things. You feel as though you have succeeded. That's not always the standard you set yourself by, but it is [the standard]. There is no gray area in football."

Another player's wife described her intense anger and disappointment after a playoff loss. "My husband looked at me and said, 'Honey, get over it. We lost.' And I said, 'That's how it is, huh? After you lose, you can't do anything about it? There is no use being upset about it?' And he says, 'You can't let it get to you. We're going to be doing this for a long time. We're going to win and lose a lot of games. You can't put all your emotions into every game.' I know this is true, but it is sooo dang hard because you want to go to the Super Bowl sooo dang bad."

Jackie Rice, who has accompanied her husband Jerry to four Super Bowls—three with the Forty-Niners and one with the Raiders—is one of the few who has perhaps earned the right to be blasé about the Super Bowl spectacle, but she says she isn't: "It is overwhelming, but at the same time you recognize that it is special. Not everyone gets the opportunity to experience that, [even] people who have been in the league for years—I think Walter Payton is someone who never got a ring. It is definitely something special."

For some, part of the excitement is undeniably monetary, because with every playoff round advancement the NFL gives all participants a bonus. In the NFL's two conferences, there are three one-game playoff rounds, and the winners in each conference meet to decide the ultimate football champion in the Super Bowl, which is held every year near the end of January.

At each playoff stage, win or lose, all players and coaches receive the same amount of money. These amounts are established in the collective bargaining agreement, and they range from approximately $15,000 to $140,000, depending on the playoff level. While these amounts might not even crease the wallets of the handful of veteran superstars, for lower-rung rookie players and assistant coaches, these extra greenbacks make a huge difference. They are sometimes seen as an overdue reward for years of toil, and NFL families are very grateful for the chance to pay off a mortgage, fix up a house, or buy a new car.

Pat Kennan recalls:

I have to say, Larry's first year with the Raiders, I really didn't understand the playoffs and all that stuff. We lost to the Jets in the second game, and I said to him, "You know, I am kind of glad the season is over." Then he said, "That cost us twenty-four thousand dollars." And I was never the same after that. Then our second year we won the Super Bowl. The other part of it was we used to go to the playoffs all the time when we were with the Raiders, and then the last years we didn't. I remember walking with another wife, and I said, "Well, I won't get new carpets this year." Because that is like your bonus, but you live on it.

And yet money isn't the real allure. It could be argued that there is no grander stage in sports than the NFL Super Bowl. It is the most widely watched event on television. To be sure, the spectacle is overdramatized, and the game itself is frequently criticized as a competitive "let-down" after all the pre-game hype, but that doesn't diminish the thrill when it's your husband on the stage, performing for hundreds of millions of people around the world. The feeling is incredible.

Or it can be one of the most anxious moments of your life.

Kim Singletary and her Hall-of-Fame husband Mike Singletary, who played his entire career as a linebacker for the Chicago Bears, attended only one Super Bowl, number XX, in 1985. The Bears won, but Kim doesn't have fond memories of the event. She recalls:

I was pregnant with our first child, and Mike was so—he was always known for his intensity. I was like: I am going to kill you. At the end of the week, he was just so ridiculously intense. He took all the pictures in his hotel room and turned them around to make them canvases to watch film. We never left the room. This is when I could visit him in his room. We had a club sandwich every day in his room because he wasn't going to leave. If I wanted to see him at all, I had to sit in there with him.

So we both say we really missed the Super Bowl. We really missed the experience: Mike from a player's perspective—he just forgot to enjoy it—and me just kind of from an emotional perspective. It is the end of the season and you are just exhausted, needing him. And you are sick of people, and there is such a frenzied hysteria in the air. It is just the greatest emotional and physical drain on a person that is possible.

Kim says Mike thought, " 'Oh, we will go back.' We never went back. As a coach, he always tells guys now: Hey, make sure you enjoy it. He forgot that."

Jackie Rice admits that going to the Super Bowl is "a lot of work." She says, "You have people coming out of the woodwork, people that you haven't spoken to since grade school; everybody is calling wanting tickets. I am like: 'Who is this?' It is kind of funny. Wives are taking on all the responsibility because you want to organize things so the guys can concentrate on the game. The way it is set up, the team leaves a whole week before the families arrive, so families are left behind dealing with everything: trying to schedule people on flights, game tickets, trying to get your kids out of school, gathering their homework from their teachers."

Asked to compare her Super Bowl experiences, Jackie says:

I think I enjoyed my second Super Bowl better than the first. The first was a bit overwhelming. My first Super Bowl, some of the wives didn't tell me as soon as you come back to your city, you immediately go to the parade. Our first Super Bowl was in Florida, and as soon as we landed back in San Francisco, you had to get on buses to go downtown to get on floats. You have this huge ticker-tape parade.

My first Super Bowl, coming home from the plane, I had an eighteen-month-old daughter; I was wearing jeans and a sweatshirt, and she was still on the bottle, so I had milk stains on my shirt. When we landed, all these wives were just so sharp—they had changed into their suits or whatever—and I was there in tears. No one had informed me. I had a baby who was cranky, I had milk stains, and here I was riding down Market Street with jeans and a jacket on. I was in tears and I was upset, and Jerry was getting upset and he was like: "You are okay, you are fine; just cover it up. Don't spoil it. Let's just try to keep this a happy occasion, okay?"

Jackie laughs at the memory. "I was just trying my darnedest not to spoil this happy occasion. But by the time the second Super Bowl came around, I was *ready*. I was ready for everything."

I accompanied my husband John and the Oakland Raider staff to Super Bowl XXXVII in San Diego, California, in 2002. Even though the Raiders lost to the Buccaneers—or, more accurately, they were crushed—I would streak naked down the 50-yard line for the chance to return (well, give me a year with *The Buns of Steel* video first). From the team-chartered "family" plane, to the Super Bowl insignia-emblazoned loaner Caddy upon my arrival, to the private, celebrity-studded parking lot tailgate, where *everything* was on the house, it is difficult to pick my favorite moment. The entire four days was a fast-paced, high-energy, nerve-wracking blur.

Though we held rooms in the same hotel, I caught only parting glimpses of my ever-working husband. The poor guy never gets to have any fun, I remember thinking as I hastily headed out to the Commissioner's Ball. Held in a gargantuan empty air force base hanger, the party included revolving drinking bars, acrobatic and live music performances in every corner, and even, in a separate room, overstuffed sofas and co-ed cage dancers. Trying her best not to stare at the impounded men, my Midwest mother was thunderstruck. She and my dad still talk about "That Room."

By game day, the preceding days' and weeks' excitement had taken a toll on me and the women around me. Some players' wives, forgetting their carefully applied mascara, bawled like babies. Others had fistfuls of cameras—disposable, digital, and video—pointed toward the field, hoping their husbands or boyfriends might glance over their way. A few coaches' wives were crouched over their children, grasping little shoulders and attempting to make eye contact. Above the pulsating noise and distractions, I imagined these mothers saying, "Remember this instant, child. This is special." Or maybe they were telling their children to be proud of their daddy, teaching their youngsters that dreams really can come true.

I remember standing on unsteady legs as I anticipated the on-coming military jets roaring past in their precise overhead columns. One hand shielded my eyes as squiggly confetti paper sprayed wildly in every possible direction. I was scanning the stadium trying to find John's press box. "My God," I remember thinking, "How can he do this? I can barely think. He has to coach this game!" The vibrating, thudding boom of the stadium cannons raised my nape hairs and furrowed sound waves deep into my stomach. If I had one word to describe the pre-kickoff atmosphere, I would have to say . . . electrifying.

Oh yeah, I want to go back. I'd consider suffering through a thirty-game football schedule with triplets to get that adrenaline rush again. Next time, however, I want to return home wearing the Wives' Pendant: the downsized Super Bowl replica ring worn on a chain and given, complimentarily, to the wives of the winning team.

What? Now You Want a Vacation?

For players and coaches—and for their wives and families—the off-season entails a lot more football than most people realize—and more than some would prefer. For wives, the off-season can also be an awkward, unsettling time of too much husband and not enough comforting routine.

Once a team's season is over, whether at the end of the regular season or after the Super Bowl, the team's overworked coaches are usually rewarded, not with a vacation, but by having their work hours scaled back to a more "normal" schedule, usually anywhere from forty to sixty hours per week; these do not include minicamps or draft preparations, when the work hours increase. Some teams give their staffs a few days off, but then it is back to work, prepar-ing for the next season. Most teams make coaches wait to take their vacations, typically until some time during the four weeks prior to training camp. Interestingly, during the first few weeks of the off-season, many wives report that it is not uncommon for their husbands to become sick, their bodies finally succumbing to illnesses they have been fighting all season.

Most coaches' wives expressed relief and joy at having their husbands back again. One woman exemplified this sentiment when she said, "During the season, we can't go on vacation. We can't go away for the weekend. We rarely even get out for dinner, let alone a movie. It gets so monotonous during the season. During the off-season, we spend a lot of family time together. We don't go places without each other, and we don't take anything for granted. Even if it is just for the night, we try to get away."

Players, particularly older, nothing-left-to-prove veterans, are afforded plenty of off-days to spend with their families in the off-season. Thrilled to no longer have to bear witness to their partners' physical abuse and grateful for a little help with the cooking, cleaning, and shopping, most players' wives look forward to this time. Most travel, whether to an off-season home or to exotic locales, and try to relax.

One player's wife says, "I love to go back home to North Carolina after the season. That's where we still keep all of our belongings and our permanent home. We get to return to our church that we love, and we have family around. The off-season is family time, and we get to take vacations. But by the end of the off-season, it is kind of nice to get away from family. I like adventure, so I do look forward to coming back out here. I love California. I just wish it were a shorter season."

Another player's wife described the off-season as "very laid back, very easy going, and basically more fun." She said she looked forward most to "having him around more when everyone is not trying to get a piece of him and take ownership. During the season I do enjoy the support, but you do have people who take ownership in him. During the off-season, I enjoy having him more to myself."

But not all players enjoy a relaxing off-season. For some, the off-season requires a trip to the operating table, and then the following months are given over to recuperation and rehabilitation. Generally, as the number of years in the league increases, so do the surgeries.

In addition, every team has an off-season workout program, which includes about a dozen scheduled "organized team activities" (called OTAs), where players work on specific plays, routes, and so on. And there are usually two minicamps. Teams "highly recommend" that their players participate in all of these activities, but usually only one minicamp is mandatory. If their husbands are not well known and highly established, however, many wives feel their partners' career would be harmed if they did not attend these "voluntary" practices. In many cases, players leave their families at their off-season homes while they return for the team's off-season workouts.

In some cases, a player's wife takes on a very active role in her husband's career, becoming something of a manager/agent for the player. For such couples, off-season days may not slow down much at all. The manager/agent organizes her partner's calendar and schedules his promotional appearances. She catches up on his fan mail and autograph signings—a few women save time by forging the player's name. Ever-vigilant of prolonging his playing career, she takes charge of the player's off-season physical condition, ordering nutritional supplements, shopping at the health food store, and preparing only performance-inducing meals.

Some women refuse to let their partners participate in any risky physical activities, or at least they try to prevent it. As one player's wife said, "I'm more worried about injuries than he is. Your job is football, and you need those legs. I've seen guys get taken out playing basketball during the off-season, and that ended their careers. My husband's theory is, 'I can get hurt just walking out the door.' "

These savvy micromanagers know that players with nonfootball injuries (NFI) can be cut at any time. Though a standard player's contract does not list any specifically prohibited activities or sports, the contract does state that the player shall not "engage in any activity other than football which may involve a significant risk of personal injury."

Not every player with an NFI is automatically let go. Players on the NFI list do not count against a team's roster, but it is up to the team to decide if it still wants to pay the player's salary when he is on the NFI. For instance, if a player comes down with an illness during the season and cannot play, the team could put him on NFI and not pay him while he is sick. Obviously, this is a potential public relations problem for teams, so most players get paid. If an injury is football related, however, the team is obligated to pay the player while he is injured and on injured reserve.

For big-name players, the off-season is frequently filled with numerous charitable events, such as golf fund-raisers and black-tie auction dinners, and these keep high-profile couples on the move, shuttling through airports and in and out of hotels. Some women enjoy this, and others report that because of it they actually prefer in-season life. These celebrity functions would seem to be the perfect, stress-free time to enjoy the glamour of NFL life, but for these women, sleeping in their own beds and counting on the weekly seasonal routine is infinitely preferable.

Of the off-season, one famous quarterback's wife says, "Sometimes I don't know where we are going or what we are doing!"

When asked what she preferred, the in-season or the off-season, Jackie Rice reflected back over seventeen years of married life:

> You know what? The first few years, I thought the in-season was more stressful because he was gone all the time; he traveled a lot and worked a lot. When you first get into it, it is like: 'I don't see you much during the season,' so in the off-season you can't wait to be together all the time.
>
> But as the years go by, it seems like things flip-flop. I enjoy the season better because I enjoy my time and my space. When you first get married, you want to spend all the off-season time together, and you still do somewhat, but you also want to get to do your own thing. You find your niche in life and the things that you like to do. The in-season allows you to have more time to do the things you like to do instead of kind of cater to someone else.
>
> Now you get so used to not being together, you start formulating your routine. And the things you like to do are not seasonal things; you like those things year round. Then the off-season begins and you are like: Okay, I need to alter the things that I usually do because this person is here more.

In fact, nearly every player's wife to whom I spoke said that having her husband home 24/7 for weeks on end was usually no picnic. For many it required adjustments they were happy to make, such as getting a little help with household chores and construction projects and perhaps reinforcing (or gaining) a measure of respect for the work *they* did as wife and mother year round.

One veteran linebacker's wife says, "During the season I understand that he's tired when he comes home—not that he doesn't still spend time with the kids. But I don't expect him to get up and do the dishes and laundry. During the off-season, though, I think he should be doing as much as I'm doing."

Jackie Rice says that one chore she and Jerry share is getting their children to school. She says, "During the season, Jerry gets up and gets the kids dressed, and I have to take them to school. Then in the off-season, we get up and get the kids dressed, and we take them together."

For some, however, having their husbands underfoot every minute can become nearly unbearable, until they get to the point where they can't wait for the season to start again. One woman wrote simply, "I love it when my partner is away. It gives me time to myself." Kathy Nolan admits that after a while she usually thinks to herself about her husband, "Okay, you are cramping my style."

Who's in charge of the house during the off-season sometimes becomes an issue, as another woman made clear:

One off-season—and I'm kind of a smart aleck—my husband was looking at the checkbook and having a fit. He said, "How do we *live?* I don't understand!" I said, "Well, I take all the bills, and I hold them over the table, and I throw them up in the air. And every one that lands on the table I pay, and those that fall on the floor I don't pay." Then I turned around and walked away.

I was so upset because he was questioning me. I have taken care of things for how many months, and he never looked at the checkbook. The lights always flicked on when he hit the switch, and the TV worked when he grabbed the remote, and he could have cared less during the season. But now that he was home, I had to account for every penny! I refused to do it. That happened almost every off-season. Then you can't wait for the minicamps to start: "Hooray for the minicamps! He is going to be gone! Hooray for the draft! He is going to be busy. He is going to be out of my hair!"

It's not always just the wife who wants the off-season to end, and the feeling is not always negative. As Barbara Flores, wife of longtime (but now retired) head coach Tom Flores, says, "I knew Tom really loved football. Every year before training camp would start, he would start getting kind of cranky, like he just couldn't wait to go play with his friends."

Sundays Are More than "Just a Game" **4**

By definition, NFL football is a game, one that's played for the entertainment of fans, and a day at the stadium is meant to be the highlight of every fan's week, or year, depending on how often he or she comes. It's a party, a social event, a show, and last but not least, a fierce, exciting competition. And all the fans, whether they are watching in person or on TV, want the same thing: big plays, big hits, and decisive victories. They want their team to win dramatically and to win every week and to do so with not a little bit of style.

For NFL women and their families, game day is something else entirely. It is certainly a social event; it is sometimes a party (if you're winning); but it is almost never just a game. NFL women get caught up in the anxious, charged atmosphere of the stadium like anybody else, but it doesn't make for a fun-filled, cathartic autumn afternoon—because the fierce competition everyone is watching involves their loved ones. A player's wife never knows at kickoff if her husband will be the one catching the game-winning touchdown or the one lying broken on the field, his and their future at the mercy of that massive hit. For a coach's wife, that day's final score might make the difference between her hard-working husband's contract being renewed or terminated immediately.

It's difficult to relax with so much at stake on every play. Some wives find it hard to watch the game at all. From the moment the day begins until the final second ticks and the game is over, an NFL woman's game-day experience is one highly emotional and stressful roller coaster.

Activity Director and Ticketmaster

It would be nice if all an NFL wife had to do was attend the game, but rather than being the one chauffeured to the stadium to watch her husband's big day, she is normally the one playing limo driver to any number of family and friends in town for the game. In fact, rare is the spouse of an NFL player or coach who escapes the dreaded twin duties: activity director and ticketmaster.

On the night before home games, players and some coaches stay in a hotel. Teams have established this policy so that everyone can concentrate on the next day's contest and not be distracted by life at home. In the morning, players and coaches drive to the stadium separately from their families, whom they will see only when the game is over.

This is smart from the NFL's perspective. The home of an NFL player or coach can become a very hectic place as game day nears. It varies, but many weekends involve one or more airport runs to gather out-of-town family and friends who have arrived to watch the upcoming game. Company is nice, but it also means coordinating and entertaining people who are themselves on vacation. Sometimes it means having them in your home, and it means hosting social events and planning stadium transportation for a handful to a dozen or more folks.

Gina Nedney, who is married to an NFL place-kicker, describes the in-season life of many NFL women when she says, "During the season, I am very busy entertaining. We have people coming in for probably every home game to watch the game. Joe is not around, so I have to clean and shop and entertain, because normally these people have never been to that state and want to see part of the state."

Part of what can turn this ongoing entertaining into a burden are the expectations and sometimes bold presumptions of the people visiting, as one player's wife made clear: "People have a tendency to just tell you what they want. If you were going to travel somewhere else or take a vacation, you would have a travel agent. It wouldn't just happen automatically. I think sometimes people just want you to make everything happen for them."

Being the social director, though, is small potatoes next to the huge headache of coordinating tickets among eager family, friends, and acquaintances. Players and coaches don't have the time or inclination to deal with it, so ticket ordering, distribution, and payment collection invariably falls to the spouses. With few exceptions, every NFL woman with whom I spoke called this the all-time biggest game-day hassle. And if the player or coach is employed by a team near the city where he grew up, the ticket situation magnifies tenfold.

The main issue is, of course, free tickets. Everybody expects or wants one, and most people are under the impression that NFL players and coaches have access to an unlimited number. In fact, free tickets are very restricted. Throughout the league, players and their families normally receive two free tickets per home game. For away games, players do not receive any free tickets. Coaches and their families usually receive four tickets for home games, and some NFL teams give their coaches a couple of free tickets to away games.

If a player or coach wants additional tickets, he has to purchase them, and he gets no discount. While he can often reserve as many extra tickets as he likes (so long as the game is not sold out), these can only be had at full price. This means that NFL wives are in almost constant negotiation with others over the cost of tickets throughout the season, and it's exhausting.

As one NFL wife says, "People don't understand that we pay for those tickets, and when people ask for something, they think you can just walk into the Chargers and they have stuff to pass out."

One player's wife has learned that "you have to say no. It is okay to say, 'We can order you tickets, and you can pay us.' And 'No, we can't fly you out here.' And 'No, we can't get you a signed Peyton Manning jersey.' It's okay to say no."

By no means all, but some people presume (and the very rude occasionally say) that because a couple is in the NFL, they must be rich, so they should pay for everyone who asks for a ticket. But the truth is that not everyone in the NFL is rich. Nor does having money mean that one is automatically obligated to pay. The NFL women to whom I spoke had a variety of responses to this attitude, but one veteran coach's wife was typical. She does not charge her close family members for tickets she has to pay for, "but when others call and say, 'Oh, my neighbor really wants to go,' I will tell them how much it costs. I don't think that is cheap. I think it would be dumb on my part not to. Because the fact is, the tickets are not free. They could be $70 a pop. When you add it up . . . . I believe we are generous to people who we want to be generous with, but I think we are also smart about not overextending ourselves."

One player's wife spoke of how hard it is to "play the bad guy" all the time, but she said, "We provided way too many tickets one year for people, and now I made a rule for next season: only parents. Everybody else has to pay for themselves."

However, setting any kind of limit inevitably leaves somebody out. The player's wife continues, "I actually had a huge run-in with one of my friends this year. They live in Michigan, and we were going to Detroit for a game. They said, 'That is one game that we could attend and meet you.' And she called at the last minute and said, 'Can we get four tickets instead of two, for my friend and her son?' And I said yeah, but they are not free. And she was appalled. 'Well, I don't think we can go then. We just assumed it was one of the perks that came along with your job.' Because it is somehow my job. It is not my job."

And where are these highly sought-after seats? Where do NFL women and families—and their friends—get to sit once they get to the stadium? A very few big-name players purchase a suite for their wives and friends, and the head coach's wife will sometimes sit in a team-provided suite with a charitable organization or local business executives. However, the vast majority of NFL women sit in the regular seats with the rest of the fans.

Family seating varies among the different teams throughout the league: it ranges from highly desirable, 50-yard-line club-level seats to those tucked in the corners of the end zone with a view partially obstructed by goalposts. In some cold-weather stadiums, teams offer a suite for the coaches' wives, and at other arenas there is a designated "family room." This is usually a place to feed and change children and get refreshments, but more often than not, it's a cramped, cinder-block-walled room under the stadium—and far from lavish.

On the Road

Because of the logistics involved, most women with whom I spoke do not bother traveling to away games. They find it easier to stay home and watch the games on TV. When NFL families do attend road games, they are more like two-day business trips than mini-vacations. Except for the occasional head coach's wife, women are not allowed to fly on the team plane, and they are on their own once they arrive in the away city. They must make their own reservations, pay for their own travel and room accommodations, and get their own transportation to the stadium. Plus, the tickets reserved for the away team are typically bad seats, high in the rafters.

This is no accident. Most teams discourage women from traveling, and management makes certain that players have little time to spend socializing or sightseeing. The minute teams arrive at the hotel, their itineraries are tightly controlled, with mandatory meals and team meetings taking up most of the day. Curfew is set at either 11:00 p.m. or midnight. It sounds silly, but players are almost literally "tucked in" at night. Two coaches walk the hallways, knocking on every player's door to ensure that he is alone and in his room. No women—no star-struck groupies or legal spouses—are allowed. If caught, players face serious fines.

After a season or two, after they realize what a no-kidding business professional football is, most wives and girlfriends quickly come to terms with the curfew and rigid scheduling during road games. They learn that sneaking into a player's or coach's room for a midnight romp could take time away from studying formations. Not executing the correct formations could mean a missed tackle. A missed tackle could mean sitting out the next game on the bench. A couple of games on the bench could mean being cut after the season.

According to one veteran player's wife:

I think one of the best things that the NFL does is have the players stay the night in a hotel the night before a game. They don't need the pressures of everyday life at home before they have to perform before seventy thousand people. I think if he was home the night before a game, and even the morning before the game, I would be doing the normal wife thing and saying, 'Will you do this? Will you do that?' instead of letting him focus. If he does come home the morning before a game, I try not to be there, or I try to let him do what he needs to do and not ask him a lot of questions and talk to him.

Many women are also afraid of the consequences if their partner is caught breaking the rules. One veteran player's wife says, "I remember for the first five years, I was afraid to go into his room at away games. I was afraid to go into the hotel because people didn't want you there. You are a distraction. I didn't want him to get in trouble. I never felt like I was welcome at any road games."

In addition, no time is wasted returning home from road games. Less than two hours after a game ends, the away team is boarding a flight home. The team's chartered plane typically arrives home hours before the women, who fly on commercial airlines. I have heard about loyal, mostly "old-school," wives who drive to the terminal in the wee hours to welcome home their warrior-husbands. But few of the NFL women to whom I spoke do this. My warrior drives his own chariot home and is cautious not to wake his sleeping beauty when he arrives.

Dressing the Part

Football fans can usually recognize the seat sections belonging to NFL families. Besides the fact that there are few men in them, the women are usually dressed differently than other fans. They aren't wearing team logo sweatshirts and track outfits.

Of course, the weather influences what women wear, but at most games, players' wives and many coaches' wives dress more formally and more stylishly than a football game normally warrants. Often they will be wearing a nice blouse with pants or designer jeans, with a matching handbag and trendy shoes. Their makeup is usually close to perfect, and if they have long hair, it is rarely worn on top of the head in a messy ponytail. Once in a while there will be a shirt with a team logo, but it is not uncommon for these women not to sport any of their team's colors.

Contrary to the stereotype, NFL women do not drip in jewels and brandish fur coats—though if caught in just the right outdoor stadium light, some veteran wives do indeed have oversized diamond rings that could blind an entire seating section. But the women still are almost never dressed like typical football fans.

The reasons for this vary widely. Some women have arrived from church, and others are dressed to go out to dinner with their partners after the game. Several women told me they dressed nicely because they felt they were representing their partners at their place of work. Rosemary Bennett, whose husband is currently a punter for the Minnesota Vikings, sounds like a typical mom in her reply: "For me, it's one day out of the week without kids, so I like to get dressed up."

One basic truth is that these women perhaps have more time and money than other women to put into their appearance, so they take advantage of that. But NFL women also said they dressed better than the average fan because they knew people would be judging them. Players' wives, in particular, feel pressure to look "the role" of the NFL wife—that is, sexy clothes, flashy jewelry, and a great body.

One NFL woman says, "You're in the pro limelight. Any woman's natural intuition is: I want to look good. I don't want to look like crap in front of these people."

Or as one player's wife says, "I want to look nice when my husband comes out of the locker room if we, you know, walk by the fans. Fans have a certain perception of NFL couples, so it's important to look nice. Some women want to be noticed, but a lot of them are really down-to-earth people."

Kim Ruddy, whose husband Tim has been a starting center for the Miami Dolphins for over ten years, put this perhaps most sharply: "Unfortunately, our world is made up of what people think of you, and I think that women in the NFL are nervous that someone is going to look down on them."

Nor is it just the fans that NFL women dress for; it is for each other as well. It is intimidating for newbie girlfriends to go from wearing puka shell necklaces and tank tops at college games to being surrounded by tennis bracelets and Coach diaper bags in the pros.

One player's wife says, "The first game I went to, I didn't want to give off the wrong impression of myself, like be too revealing. Some people will come in, and you're thinking, 'Are you going to the club, or are you going to a football game?'"

Some NFL women use material possessions to communicate their status level within the league. A high-profile, highly paid veteran player's or coach's wife has tremendous pressure to dress to her husband's elevated position. Like other rich folks, sometimes NFL women have their self-esteem and self-worth wrapped up in their material possessions, and there exists an underlying competition in clothes, jewelry, and fashions. One veteran wife admitted, "I think there is a little bit of 'I am better than you.' I am wearing Manolos; those look like they came from Target."

One rookie player's wife was honest and self-aware in her observations: "Some people have beautiful jewelry, really pretty jewelry, and normal people don't wear that type of jewelry. As a woman, I think you are just naturally drawn to beauty, and there is that jealousy that, I think, can spark in just about anyone. It's a pressure I think that we each put on ourselves, and it really has a lot to do with your self-confidence and whether you really want to compete or not. But when you're pulled back down to reality, it's a different thing. I appreciate a lot of things that other wives can wear, but then you think to yourself, it's not necessarily where I'm at right now, and it's not important."

She concluded with an interesting insight that places part of the responsibility for a woman's self-confidence on NFL men: "The way you dress can also reflect how good your husband makes you feel about yourself. I think the husbands can put some pressure on the wives to look a certain way or do certain things because they may be insecure with themselves."

The bigger and more well-known the player or coach, the more attention his wife or girlfriend will receive. And yet the longer women spend in the league, typically the less they feel the need to play a role or compete with other women.

One veteran NFL wife offered this advice to women new to the NFL: "Don't change or don't feel that you need to play the part of an

NFL wife because there is no specific part to play. Just be yourself. I've struggled with that. Should I dress up? Should I get a bigger ring? You do waiver, and that is okay."

As the spouse of a famous Hall of Fame player, Kim Singletary has had to deal with the expectations put on her by others, as well as those she has put on herself. Today, she says, "I have had to sort of teach myself that my self-worth and my value to society are not based on how people look at me and treat me. When your husband is in his heyday, people treat you like, Who is she? Unless you are the prettiest of the Barbies, unless you are that top girl, it is always like you are less than somebody. I have had to learn that my value is not tied up in how people treat me or look at me, or even talk about me or what they think I should be like. I really had to go to school on myself for that one."

Bracing for the "Kill Shot"

Every other game-day hassle and worry, however, pales beside the fear that your partner will get hurt.

Kim Ruddy says, "Even to this day, I go out there and I sit down and think, 'Please, God.' Every week, every game, every hit, I think, 'Just get up.'"

I was singing the same hymn when John lay motionless after getting blown up on a kickoff return while playing in the Canadian Football League. Someone missed a block, and he got blasted. Horrified, I watched as his torso flew backward, cleats and hips parallel to the turf. He was airborne fifteen feet before landing on his left shoulder, with his head bouncing to a standstill.

When he didn't get up, the referee called a time-out. The trainers rushed over, and through the jumble of arms, legs, and medical equipment, my eyes zeroed in for a twitch of movement. Nothing. I felt my throat start to close. In a frightened stupor, I left my seat and descended to the bottom row of the bleachers, where the steel railing stopped me. My face was burning hot. The pale yellow turtleneck I wore squeezed like a torture device. Twenty seconds passed as I stood there, frozen, staring at John's still body.

As I focused on John, I heard the crowd exclaim in unison, "Ohhh!" and then "Aaahh" several times, until I followed the crowd's gaze up toward the JumboTron. After replaying the slow-motion image of my best friend and lover torpedoing into green Astroturf, the camera panned to a live close-up—of me! There I was, red-cheeked and yanking at the sweater around my throat, my eyes bright with unshed tears.

Seeing my overblown face on a 20 x 20-foot screen almost pushed me over the edge—literally. I grabbed the bleacher railing and started to climb over, determined to run onto the field and get to John, when he pulled up his knee. The trainers helped him to his feet, and only after they had coaxed him to the sidelines did my throat finally stop constricting and I let go of the metal bar in my hands.

As I headed back to my seat, I heard several excited comments: "That boy got his ass knocked off!" "Wow, what a kill shot!" And, "He sure got 'de-cleated!'"

I never want to feel that terrified or helpless again. After that incident, my throat would start to tighten every time John suited up. I didn't mind in the least when John "retired" and started coaching.

Unfortunately, the wife of nearly every player has a similar story to tell. A running back's wife relates the following:

> During the game I am always anxious because he is always getting hit. I'm always making sure he gets up. I'm excited when he is doing everything, but when they all pile up on him, I just keeping thinking, "Get up already." He is going to be on the bottom. If he goes down and doesn't get up, I'm going down.
>
> It happened last year. He was hit and he didn't get up. I ran all the way from the suite and around, and he still didn't get up. I ran all the way down on the field and got on the field, and they said he had gone to have X-rays. So I ran back up, and I met him right as he was coming in. I cried and cried. I was all upset because he couldn't walk. I rode in the ambulance with him and stayed with him at the hospital.

Another player's girlfriend described what it was like being in the stadium when her boyfriend took one of those quintessential big hits:

I was sitting with my brother, and I saw my boyfriend get whacked. He looked like he had taken a really hard hit, but he jumped right back up. But my brother said, "Whoa, that was huge, that was a huge deal." And they paused the game for a minute. Apparently he could have been paralyzed really easily from that hit. He jumped right back up, but it was a really big penalty on the play, and the guy who did it got fined fifty thousand dollars.

And the guy behind me starts yelling, "Yeah, stop making a big deal. It is football. Let them play, let them play. Get your ass back on the field." All because they paused for a minute.

It is hard 'cause I see him get battered and bruised, and I am who he is with when he comes home from the game. He's always got injuries, you know. Not huge ones, but little stuff that, for me, I would be crying to the emergency room about, you know?

Another wife spoke about her emotions and her literal need for faith: "I have watched him go down on the field, and he ended up having a concussion. It's a panic or tightness around my heart just waiting for some sign to see exactly what it is. More so, it's just a feeling of uneasiness, and usually the first thing that comes to me is to start praying that it's not as bad as it looks. It's not a good feeling. But I rarely dwell on it because I pray before every game. Usually, I pray for him on the way to the game, as well as for his teammates. A lot of times when I get there, I also pray for the other team."

The wife of a wide receiver says she worries less about injuries if she does not watch her husband directly on the field. Instead, if she watches at all, she looks at the television in her stadium suite.

She says, "My mom is in the front of the suite by the window, and she is hollering and telling me what is happening, but I watch the screen more than I watch him on the field. Most of the time, I'll get up and socialize and entertain rather than watch the game. People will say, 'Did you see your husband run in for the touchdown?' and I go, 'Oh, I missed it.' I just feel more secure like that."

The wife of a running back prepares for game-day violence by hyping up. She says, "I listen to the radio on the way there, even if it's just church songs with the kids, and get myself as excited as I can be to go out and watch them get pounded. It's rough, and you have to be ready for it. When they get hit, you have to be ready."

A Ticket Stub and Garlic Fries: A License to Abuse

In her first few years in the league, when she was younger and had "more blood flowing," Kim Ruddy would get extremely irritated with loudmouthed fans who criticized her husband as he was playing. The former model and tennis instructor describes her most notorious moment, when she actually punched a fan in the nose:

> He was sitting in front of me, and he was being really obnoxious and really rude about the offense. He obviously knew who I was because he said a couple of times, "Ruddy sucks!" right in my face. I asked him politely a couple of times to keep his verbal abuse to himself and said that I was just there to watch the game. He kept going and going, and then I said, "Sir, you really do need to keep it to yourself." Then he looked at me and said, "I don't know who the fuck you think you are," and he got right in my face and he shoved my shoulder. That's when I clocked him.
>
> He was a little shocked. He gave me a look, and then he came at me like he wanted to hit me back. Then I called the security guard down and asked him to remove the guy.

Kim says the fans around her "weren't surprised" the loudmouth got hit. "The guy was obnoxious the whole game. I think they were just waiting for someone to clock him, but I don't know if they really realized that it was going to be me." Kim laughs, adding, "The guy was going to get clocked by someone before the game was over."

Even after ten years of watching Tim's games, Kim remains passionate and protective of her husband. Like a number of women with whom I spoke, Kim does not hesitate to defend the one she loves, though she has toned down a bit.

She says, "These days, I'm just kind of like, 'Maybe you should be careful what you say because you never know who is sitting around you. Just keep it to yourself.' Fans are usually not very nice when I say something to them. Fans have their opinions on how a guy should play and how they played high school football. If they were as good as they talk in the stands, they would be out there."

Most NFL women realize that for football fans, voicing their displeasure as well as their excitement is part of the game. Even the injury-causing violence that makes NFL wives shudder is part of the "entertainment" of football. Fans come to have a good time, and these things are part of it. As Pat Kennan says wryly, "Fans like to second-guess."

Unfortunately, some fans do more than just criticize the play-calling or briefly boo a costly mistake. They belittle and berate. They disparage and attack and punish. They get personal and just plain nasty.

College football crowds can be just as rowdy, but they are not as aggressive as NFL fans can be. The girlfriend of an NFL player says, "I think fans in the NFL will turn on you much faster. They don't have a personal attachment [as do college fans who] went to that college for four years."

Another player's girlfriend, who was used to her university's winning ways and undying fan support, said she had a hard time her first year in the NFL: "I remember my first game. I couldn't believe the things that were being said. I take everything very personally, and I would get myself in trouble. I would verbally react. I remember once my boyfriend had a less than stellar game snapping, and a man coming up the aisle was saying something about him, and I reacted without even thinking. I feel very protective of him and my friends."

The higher your profile and responsibility on the team, the more likely you are to be noticed, by either cheers or boos. Among coaches, usually only the head coach and sometimes the offensive and defensive coordinators get singled out for haranguing. Likewise, unknown or low-profile players often escape the verbal barrage that might hound a quarterback or star defensive back.

Women react differently, based on their personalities and the situations. All women said that abuse directed at their team made them uncomfortable. What is hard to swallow without comment is a personal attack on the person with whom they share their lives. And what infuriates wives most of all is when their children are with them and hearing the abuse, particularly once they are old enough to realize what is being said about their daddies.

Some women, like Kim Ruddy, don't hesitate to give it back to fans who cross the line. Others said they would respond only if a fan attacked a player by name, and then sometimes only if the player's family was sitting nearby and could overhear. These women said they try to defuse the situation by politely informing the abusive fans that they are sitting in a family section and that the player's or coach's wife or child could be sitting nearby.

However, some women said they would never return fire with a fan. The last thing they want is for the fan to know they are affiliated with the team. Kori Shaw, wife of a Baltimore Ravens assistant position coach, says, "If they know who I am, it can be directed at me, and then it becomes personal."

Some women didn't want to deal with unpredictable drunks. The wife of a player told the story of arriving at a game after a charity event still wearing a T-shirt with her husband's name on it. After her husband drew a penalty for holding, she said three men sitting a couple of rows behind her "screamed at" and "humiliated" her. Since then, she hides the fact that she is an NFL woman.

She says, "The scary thing is that you don't know what a fan is going to do. You don't know which ones are so into it, and they get so mad. If you are walking to your car and have paraphernalia on that has your husband's name on it, and you have kids with you . . . I just don't think it's safe."

Another reason many women gave for not "getting into it" with fans was that they felt that ticket holders say things because they get caught up in the heat of the moment and that, in any case, these people are entitled to their opinions. Some NFL women also believe that wives and girlfriends "embarrass themselves" when they get into "screaming matches."

One All-Pro player's wife says, "One minute the player may have a missed tackle or a dropped pass or whatever, and the fans are going to say things. Then, when the team wins, fans are back saying that guy is their favorite player. You can't take it personally."

Lori Warhop, wife of an assistant position coach, echoes this sentiment:

I think people that purchase a ticket come to a game and they have expectations. If those expectations are not fulfilled . . . . It's just like going to a movie. You are watching the whole time, and then you're disappointed at the outcome: "I can't believe they killed him off in the end!"

Maybe they're a little upset about a loss, but they do not know my husband personally. I think there is a little ignorance there. They probably have no idea the number of hours he spends in the office working. I feel like, if they knew him personally and if they knew how hard he worked, they would probably think twice before making a comment like that.

Fantasy Football vs. Real Life

Women rarely show it, but inside the butterflies are zipping about faster than a "Viper right, F short, 772 Falcon halfback burst." How could they not feel tense? On top of all the other worries and stresses of game day, they know that poor play or a loss could spell the end of their partner's job.

There is no middle ground in football. You either win or you lose. After a loss, fans don't give a damn how many towels a player soaked with sweat in the weight room during the off-season. Likewise, when the scoreboard tally comes up short, the team's owner could care less about the piles and piles of videotapes that coaches viewed in preparation. They may as well have been watching *Disney's Most-Beloved Classics* for all that it matters.

Many fans have an emotional stake in "their" team's game, and maybe a financial one, such as a small wager with friends. For NFL families, the stakes are much higher. For a player who has not yet made the team, one day's performance, or lack thereof, could make the difference between whether or not the couple has health insurance at the time their baby is born. A key loss for a coach might mean that he is fired, which means finding another job in another city, which means, once again, uprooting the couple's children in the midst of the school year.

According to a veteran coach's wife, "It used to be that if you had a good season, that was important. Now it's how far you go in the playoffs. For some teams, if you don't win the Super Bowl, you are not good enough and you are gone. That's not a realistic expectation, and that's a lot of stress to live under."

Gina Nedney admits to feeling a lot of pressure during the game:

I probably get more nervous than both he and the rest of his family put together, because I'm a person who likes to be in control. I can't control what he does or what the team does. It's up to him and his abilities.

I think quarterbacks and place-kickers are in a very similar spotlight. A quarterback can throw a good pass, but the receiver can drop it, so it wouldn't necessarily be the quarterback's fault. When a place-kicker goes up to perform and kicks a field goal, no one sees if it was a good snap or a bad hold. All they see is if the kick is good or not good.

It's interesting, sitting in the stands. If he makes a kick, it's like, "Way to go!" and they're patting me on the back. If he misses, I don't get anyone saying anything or touching me. Every time he comes up and it's a big kick, I feel a lot of pressure.

Despite their usually reserved exteriors, many NFL women admit that it can be hard to control their emotions. A twenty-year veteran coach's wife says she has burst into tears after a badly needed touchdown. "I cannot keep my heart from beating rapidly," she says.

Some women relieve tension by yelling at the refs, but they are careful not to voice any negatives about specific players. The wife of a lineman puts it plainly: "The hardest thing is when a person on the team makes mistakes over and over, and you want so badly to scream at him, but his sister is probably sitting next to you."

When things go well on the field, NFL women try to stay just as calm; few actually get out of their seats and whoop it up. Kim Ruddy says:

I think the wives are more conservative. I think when it comes to getting down and dirty, standing up, doing the dance and screaming, "Who let the dogs out?," I don't think we do that. Once in a while the game gets so exciting you can't help yourself. But a lot of times we're so much more reserved because of public opinion. I think the public wants to see how you act, and if they know who you are, they're going to watch every move you make. If you're not reserved, they're going to be, "Oh my gosh, did you see Kim Ruddy? She was going crazy." Most of the wives sit in their seats, keep their mouths shut, and watch the game.

At times, how they handle their game-day stress can make NFL women appear quite strange to fans. These women may be attending the game but acting like they are somewhere else entirely. If you see a woman in the stands reading, as Kori Shaw does to divert her stress—she says she feels "physical pain" because of what happens on the field—you may be observing a woman who cares so much about the game's outcome that she can't watch.

Kori recalls that she was reading a magazine when the fan behind her said, "Hey, you need to stand up and cheer."

I just looked at him and kept on reading. He said, "Hey, what are you reading?" I showed him what I was reading, and he commented again. Then he leaned over and put his hand on my shoulder. I really don't like that kind of interaction with people, so I turned around and I asked him to please leave me alone. He didn't realize that I was very serious. Finally, my brother-in-law turned around and asked him to leave me alone.

The funny part of the story is that afterwards we had a post-game team dinner and that man happened to be there. When he realized that I was affiliated with the team, he apologized to me. I was fine. I wasn't mad. I just wanted to be left alone.

According to a veteran coach's wife, alcohol also does a good job of calming frayed game-day nerves, and not a few NFL women admitted to taking the edge off with a drink, albeit carefully. She spoke about the "medicinal uses of chardonnay":

For very tense and emotional games it is easier if you have a glass of wine. The older I get, the more stressed out I get. The NFL is more stressful than college because it's like right off the bat somebody scores, and somebody comes back and scores. You score. They score. It's like a nail-biter maybe all but three games a year. NFL teams are becoming more competitive because of the salary cap and player movement. You never know what is going to happen until the clock runs out.

As a wife, you sit there knowing if you don't win, things are going to change, so it makes your life more drastic. I don't know how I would get through it without a glass . . . or two.

Pulling Off the Pads and Removing the Headset

Unless the team has just won a big playoff game, NFL couples don't usually whoop it up around town after games. Kim and Tim Ruddy have a standing date to go out for sushi. Other couples pick up their children from the sitter, order takeout dinner, watch the football highlights on television, and go to bed.

Typically, it is only some of the single guys who put on their snazziest suits and head out to the exclusive VIP nightclubs after games. NFL couples, instead, will mill around in their private parking lot after games and socialize, or they will go out to dinner with other NFL couples. A few teams in the league, such as the Raiders, host a private team dinner following the team's home games. Raider women appreciate this time to unwind with family, visit with guests, and, best of all, forget about going home to cook.

One linebacker's wife sounds like any other mom in her after-game scenario: "I usually leave the girls with a babysitter, so after games we are in kind of a hurry to get home. I know some people that go out and do dinner or go out and have a good time, but most guys I know are tired and beat up, and they just want to sit down and regroup and relax."

For coaches, the Sundays following a home game are almost always "family night," since it is one of the coaches' rare nights at home. For both players' and coaches' families, the night almost always concludes with ESPN highlights from throughout the league. Everybody wants to know how the competition fared that day.

When asked if their post-game activities varied depending on whether their team won or lost, most women said no. Though the outcome of the game does not typically change their plans, the mood is definitely affected.

After a win, for one night at least, the pressure is off. One player's girlfriend says, "When they win, he is more fun because he can let things go. He is not thinking, thinking, thinking."

More than one NFL woman admitted that winning streaks were better for the couple's sex life. With a wink, one wife told me, "Wins seem to carry over to every aspect of our life. *Everything* is better after a win."

Of course, every loss has a negative effect, and no matter how well someone may have played or performed individually, everyone on the team feels it. The head coach may be the one to answer to the media and the team's owner, but it doesn't take long for the assistant coaches and all the players to feel the trickle-down effect. However, according to the women to whom I spoke, it is the rare player or coach who responds by becoming visibly, demonstrably upset or acting short-tempered with his wife or children.

According to one position coach's wife, losing games mean "shorter and quieter" post-game dinners. "My husband takes everything very personally and to heart. Even a win is hard for my husband if his players haven't played to their potential and done their assignments. I'm a lot more on edge if he's on edge."

Another coach's wife offered what most agreed was the typical, seasoned approach to winning and losing: "Sure, winning does make everything that much better. But I am always keeping in mind that this is one game out of . . . how many more do I have? We try to keep it really balanced on both sides—the winning and the losing."

No matter what the game's outcome, no one with the team—neither the players nor the coaches—stays in a bad mood for long. I find it amusing that fans are often more upset after a loss than are the game's participants. Some fans will even call in sick to work the next day because they are so distraught, whereas players and coaches rarely dwell on their setbacks. They don't have time. They have only seven days to prepare for the next game. Some coaches will go home and begin looking at film of the next opponent almost immediately following the game!

Like players and coaches, NFL women do not have time to dwell on the negatives of games past. We have too much to organize, arrange, and worry about for next Sunday's game. How are we going to manage three airport pickups in two days with a teething baby in the backseat? If my husband doesn't play well next week, will the team renew his contract? Will the jerk who called him "worthless" at the last game be sitting in our section again? Will our kid's teacher's brother actually pay for his tickets this time?

Ah, game day. Relaxing and pleasant? Not usually. Exciting and full of drama? Almost always.

1. Kori Shaw with
her daughter, Keegan,
Baltimore Ravens.
*(Photo courtesy of
Kori Shaw)*

2. Julianne Player,
Arizona Cardinals.
*(Photo courtesy
of Julianne Player)*

3. Kim Ruddy,
Miami Dolphins.
*(Photo courtesy
of Kim Ruddy)*

4. Chandra Hollier
with her husband,
Dwight Hollier.
*(Photo courtesy
of Chandra Hollier)*

5. Kathy Waufle with her husband, Mike Waufle,
New York Giants. (Photo courtesy of Kathy Waufle)

6. Gina Nedney with her daughter, Gabby,
Tennessee Titans. (Photo courtesy of Gina Nedney)

7. Susan May with her children, Lindsay-Catherine and Deems. *(Photo courtesy of Susan May)*

8. Lori Warhop, Dallas Cowboys. *(Photo courtesy of Lori Warhop)*

9. Jackie Rice,
Oakland Raiders.
*(Photo courtesy
of Jackie Rice)*

10. Kim Singletary,
Baltimore Ravens.
*(Photo courtesy of
Kim Singletary)*

11. The author poses next to her Super Bowl–
issued Cadillac. *(Author's collection)*

12. The author playing ticketmaster for the
ultimate game, Super Bowl xxxvii (with sister,
Jennifer O'Toole) *(Author's collection)*

13. The Coach's Kid, Tierney Rose Morton.
(Photo by Mickey Elliot, used with permission)

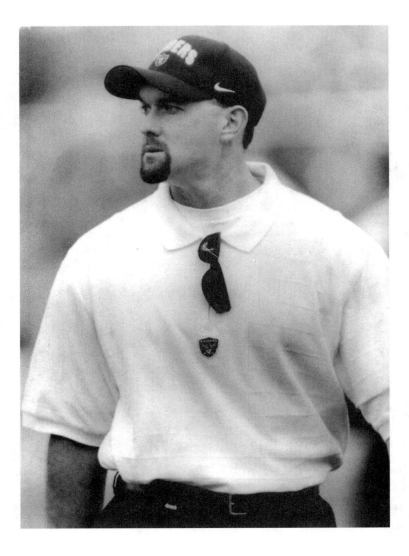

14. Coach John Morton on game day.
(Photo by Mickey Elliot, used with permission)

A Woman in a Man's Game **5**

NFL women work hard and sacrifice much to ensure that their partners first attain and then retain their careers. However, the more difficult question that NFL women face is not whether they should make those sacrifices — for almost without exception the women to whom I spoke said they were quite willing and even happy to do what was needed to help their husbands achieve success. Rather, having done that, the question that truly challenges these women is how to maintain a sense of self and personal pride when everything they see, hear, and read praises their partners and their NFL jobs and leaves the women's contributions virtually invisible.

The majority of NFL women are young — in their twenties and thirties. Most are college-educated and trained to follow a specific career path. However, even for the most career-minded women, it was almost impossible to maintain a career while married to an NFL player or coach. The demands of NFL life are too great. In fact, most women don't try. They decide to give up their careers once their husbands makes it in the NFL, or at the very least they delay them until the NFL no longer dominates their lives.

Modern young NFL women find themselves in a strange position, at least by today's standards: full-time wife and mother. Where once society expected women to take on this traditional role without question, in the NFL it continues as a matter of practical survival. During the season, NFL players and coaches are consumed by the demands of their job. As a result, even though most NFL men know how to push a vacuum, wash a load of laundry, and change diapers—and many men will say they value these things, no longer automatically assuming that every household and childrearing duty is the woman's "job"—NFL women wind up having to do them almost entirely by themselves. Considering the value our culture places on one's having a career and the enormous amount of attention that NFL players and coaches receive because of theirs, it should be no surprise that issues of self-worth and self-identity become central for NFL women.

It is easy for an NFL wife to become dependent on her partner, especially when his job moves them around so often and they live far from other family members. The player or coach can become the main person in the woman's life. For some, particularly women who are themselves very traditional or perhaps those who have never had career aspirations, the fact that everything is "just about him" can become a habit. These women start to believe that when the coach or player is home, it is their "job" to take care of him, and they identify completely with their partners' roles and NFL status.

Perhaps surprisingly, this happens much more rarely than one might think—at least judging by the responses of the women with whom I spoke. Most NFL women said they felt they could separate their own identity from their partners' jobs, and they made the point, in dozens of ways, that their pride in their partners and their genuine interest in the game of football did *not* mean they had lost their sense of self.

Veteran NFL women are a remarkably poised, confident, and self-reliant group. Attributes like these are usually earned through the trials and triumphs of one's job experiences. NFL women earn them by surviving the NFL.

A Hall of Fame Career

Like so many NFL couples, Kim Courtley met her future husband, Mike Singletary, when both were college students, and the story of their courtship in 1978 at Baylor University is told in chapter 1.

What sets Kim and Mike apart from most NFL couples—indeed, what separated them from most romantic couples in America at the time—is that Kim is white and Mike is African American. For any pair of teenagers in the South in those days, this fact alone might have been insurmountable for any relationship except the most chaste friendship.

At first, Kim and Mike were just friends. They both came from religious homes, and they found they saw life the same way, but any budding attraction they felt was kept firmly in check by the era's social realities.

Kim says, "I am not a trailblazer. I do not have the pioneer spirit. At first, we had such a deep friendship because in my mind it was not going to go any further than that, because I cannot be with a black guy. It wasn't ever stated by my parents, but it was just understood."

When Kim went home for the summer after her freshmen year, she dated other boys, but none, she found, measured up to Mike. She says, "I kept feeling, 'Dang, I wish he were more like Mike.' I got a little panicky; [I thought] I think I like him, but I don't know what to do with that."

Kim says that Mike was also "being torn in different directions." It was obvious that Baylor's star linebacker was going to be drafted into the NFL, and the people surrounding him said that his NFL career would be harmed if he continued to see Kim, but after that summer the relationship had developed into a romance. They said he wouldn't get signed to a big contract and his endorsements would suffer. Some of them even said, "If you are going to be in the NFL, you can't have a white wife. You need to marry a black girl, but keep the white girl on the side." Kim says, "But Mike knew enough to know that was wrong."

At the same time, some members of Mike's family were also against the relationship. Kim remembers, "They were telling him, 'You know the girl is not going to leave her family. So she will probably end up leaving you, and then she will take all your money.'"

Kim says that Mike kept breaking up with her, but he also kept coming back. She says, "He was getting conflicting messages. He went to his pastor—an old Pentecostal black man, Elder Perry. The pastor said, 'Do you love her? Does she love you? And does she love the Lord?' And Mike said, 'Yes.' Then the elder said, 'So what's the problem?' Mike said, 'Well, 'cause she is white.' And Elder Perry said, 'So what's the problem?' "

Mike also consulted a coach at Baylor who was white, and the coach told him, "I would have to say this: your relationship with Kim has really forced me to look at biracial relationships. I don't think of Kim as one of these gold digger girls, and if I had a man like you for any of my girls, I would have to give it my blessing."

Admitting that she prefers "smooth sailing waters," Kim was not confident that she and Mike could conquer the difficulties involved in an interracial relationship. But the two of them share a deep, abiding faith in God, and she says, "I believe God's hand was in the whole thing, so I sort of was willing to trust Him."

In addition, the teenager had more gumption than she credits herself. Kim says, "I remember at the time that I refused to just cave. I refused to go home and go to Michigan State, and I refused to stay in the room down my parents' hall where it is all nice and safe. I had a tiny bit of fight left in me, so regardless, I thought, I was sticking this out."

The couple has done much better than just sticking it out. Mike was drafted by the Chicago Bears, and over twelve seasons with the team—for whom he played his entire career—he became a perennial All-Pro linebacker, won a Super Bowl, and was inducted into the Pro Football Hall of Fame. The couple found a way to survive the turbulent first few years of his career, and today, in addition to many other accomplishments, Kim and Mike have seven children and have been married for over twenty-five years. After being retired for ten years, Mike returned to football as the linebacker coach for the Baltimore Ravens in 2002.

When asked how she has maintained her sense of self in the face of her husband's tremendous career, Kim first sighs but then is refreshingly honest in her reply: "I might be one of the casualties, because really I didn't. Everything was filtered through his schedule, his opinion, his time, his feelings, his physical body, his moods—everything was filtered through him. I maintained our marriage, at times at the expense of myself. I allowed him to make everything about him." She continues:

I never had problems being called, "the wife." I hear these young girls complain about that, and when they ask me about it, I will say, if you want the honest-to-God truth, it is like trying to turn around the Titanic. You are going to fight yourself. You just need to accept it isn't about you right now. The fans, it will not be about you. The team, it will not be about you. His schedule, it will not be about you. His coaches, it will not be about you.

My friends and my family, most of whom were not in football—they were about the only place where it was about me. The other 98 percent of my life, it was about him. It is kind of like acceptance. You are going to be so much better off if you just accept it. Forever? No. But for however long his NFL career is, this is just how it is. You cannot change the fans' perspective. They worship him. You know his faults, and you know you write all his letters, but they don't care. They worship him. I just thought, why fight it? I hear girls now say, I just want to have my own identity. I just think, okay, then you shouldn't have married him. You have his identity.

Kim admits that she and Mike hold more traditional and even old-fashioned views on marriage and gender roles, and yet her perspective has shifted over time. This became clear when Mike retired from his playing career. Kim elaborates:

When he was playing, it wasn't like I was every day consciously saying, okay, for the good of this marriage. . . . I allowed it intentionally without the awareness I have now. I knew that he was giving me his best, which now, looking back, wouldn't have been good enough. When he retired from playing, I saw how much more he is capable of.

I always say, after retirement he took his helmet off, literally and figuratively, and his eyes were more open to his family. He had his football helmet on from the day I met him. Guys don't have the best vision in that helmet. They can see a lot, but their peripheral vision is not that good because they are wearing this big helmet.

He saw us, the kids and me. And at that point, not literally, but I started saying, look, I have needs, I have interests, I have desires. I am not saying it is all about me, but I am saying it's going to be like 50/50 here, you know. Not all you.

Kim says it took perhaps five years for things to change, during which "we all had to retrain his energy. I really had to train him to see me, see a different side of me, see my gifts, see my talents. He had just been so used to looking at everything from his perspective."

In 1994, by the time Mike was eligible for the Pro Football Hall of Fame, it was obvious that he had already come to see his wife in a new light. Bestowing on her one of the highest honors in sports, Mike became the only husband ever to ask his wife to give his introduction speech. Kim says that this was Mike's way of "honoring me."

Among the words she spoke as she introduced her husband that day, Kim said, "His induction to the Pro Football Hall of Fame is an incredible honor. But I know that Mike will consider himself a success only when each of our children, after they are grown, will look back on their relationship with Mike and name him to the Fathers' Hall of Fame." Kim says:

It was another trailblazing moment, and that is not in my nature. I know there were guys that didn't like the fact that it was like a boys' club and now a wife was in there. I just felt it was this final little blessing on his career. He is kind of like the little engine that could. He was supposed to be too small, too slow, too stupid to play middle linebacker, because that was like the white, thinking, smart guys' position. He kind of broke the mold. He has the trailblazing spirit, not me. When you are that, you face persecution at times. I just felt like that was justice. I felt like God honored him. In the trump card of ways. He never looks back on that time, and he almost acts like he forgets, but I just think of how so many guys strive for that and God just gave it to him, his first year. See how blessed you are, I tell him.

Job Wanted: Six Months per Year,
No Tuesdays, Sundays, or Friday Afternoons

Kim Singletary's strength and determined spirit are obvious, despite the fact that even today she is reluctant to credit herself with these qualities. Her story also exemplifies a shift in the last two decades in the NFL and in society. Though Kim did not grow up with any particular career aspirations, women today do, and yet, as Kim says, the effort it takes to pursue one's personal goals in an NFL household is like "trying to turn around the Titanic." Some NFL women try to work and to keep their career aspirations on course, but after a time they realize that the current is perpetually against them.

For Chandra Hollier, whom we first met in chapter 1, there was simply no question that she would continue with her career as a doctor, no matter what her husband did for a living. That her husband turned out to be a linebacker for the Miami Dolphins didn't change her plans, and Chandra and Dwight spent their entire courtship and early marriage living in separate households while they independently pursued their careers. However, once Chandra finished her OB/GYN residency in Pittsburgh, she eagerly accepted a full-time job with a practice in West Palm Beach. The couple was thrilled, for at last they would be able to live together under one roof.

Then, before the start of the next season, the Dolphins decided not to re-sign their eight-year veteran. While Dwight was elated that the Indianapolis Colts showed immediate interest and signed him to a contract, it also meant the couple would be pulled apart again. Only now it was Chandra who was committed to living in Florida.

At the end of Dwight's first year with the Colts, the moving boxes were pulled out once again when Chandra quit her job to move up to Indianapolis. Unfortunately, however, increasing injuries and age had caught up with the free agent, and he was not re-signed at the end of that summer's training camp. At that point, in part to be close to Chandra's parents, the couple decided to move to Albemarle, North Carolina. Chandra found another medical practice, and Dwight began a second career working as a mental health counselor for adolescents.

There is no doubt Chandra is an extraordinary woman. She successfully pursued a long-distance NFL relationship while also taking on the grueling hours and workload required of a doctor-in-training. But her choices entailed sacrifices she hadn't expected, and not everyone around the couple — particularly some of Dwight's more traditional teammates — was supportive.

"Instead of birthing other people's children, I would have her at home birthing mine" was a comment Chandra overheard one evening while dining with other NFL couples. It exemplified an attitude both she and Dwight encountered over the years.

Chandra is now the mother of a toddler. When asked to reflect on her early years, she becomes pensive. "I never thought that I could not do what I wanted, family-wise and in school too. Now I realize there are two different tracks: the married motherhood road and the professional career road. I didn't even think about the two not meshing . . . but that was a fairy tale."

Chandra echoes the quandary all professional women face. Though Chandra doggedly maintained her course and achieved her vocational goals, generally for NFL women this is extremely difficult. Most of them will not work outside the home during their partners' NFL careers, and the ones to whom I spoke expressed several reasons for such a decision. Some want to take full advantage of what is most often a short-lived NFL opportunity. This was true for Julianne Player, who decided to postpone her career as a broadcast journalist when her husband Scott signed on as a punter with the Arizona Cardinals.

Julianne says, "I found out we would have an opportunity to do things that we might not normally get to do, like travel in the off-season and attend different events during the year. So was I going to try to find a job and not be able to do these things? Or was I going to enjoy all the benefits and any extras that come along with his job? Scott and I chose that I wouldn't work so that we could do those things together, because you never know how long you're going to be in the NFL."

Nevertheless, Julianne says that her first year in the NFL was the most difficult. Up to then a busy, career-driven woman, she wasn't satisfied sitting home while her husband went off to work, and not contributing financially to the family made her feel "unproductive." Still, her voice carries no regrets when she says, "Somebody has to sacrifice. That was a hard thing for me to do because I assumed that I would go to college, graduate, get my career going, and then settle down. It didn't happen in that order."

In contrast, other women felt fortunate that their partners were making enough money so that they could stay home and care for their children full-time. Even a modest NFL paycheck is usually much bigger than anything the wife might earn.

One player's wife says, "Right now, I'm really content to be home and be here when my husband comes home, to have dinner ready and to take care of our daughter."

For women who do want a career, probably the biggest challenges of NFL life are the frequent moves and the partners' long and/or unusual work hours. For players and their families, it is common to split residences between an in-season and an off-season home. It's not easy to find a job if women are honest with employers and admit they will be able to work only for four to six months. A lot of companies believe it takes that long just to get the hang of things.

Moreover, if an NFL player's wife wanted to see her husband during the season, she would need to inform a potential employer: "I want all of Tuesday and Friday afternoon off, and I don't want to work on Sundays." That kind of flexibility is rare in any serious, professional job. But without it, a wife working full-time outside the home and a husband with an unusual schedule would spend very little time together. As for a coach's wife, she hardly sees her husband during the season anyway, so pursuing a full-time career wouldn't necessarily mean she would see him less; rather, her challenges would arise with her partner's frequent job relocations.

Another problem with wives and girlfriends working outside the home is the constant possibility that a player may become severely injured. After he has surgery to repair whatever torn body part needs fixing—a hip, groin, arm, wrist, or whatever—his wife often doubles as his rehabilitation specialist. For many gridiron veterans, this applies to the off-season as well, which usually includes at least one trip under the knife. One lineman's wife was forced to quit her job because her employer did not understand why she was taking so many days off. She needed to be home to help her invalid husband-athlete dress and bathe and to drive him to doctors' appointments.

The other major challenge, the almost continuous need to move, also wreaks havoc with work schedules. Nonestablished, "journey-men"-type players, who constitute a huge chunk of players in the NFL, are constantly shuffling between teams, sometimes more than once a year. For NFL coaches, frequent moves are an unwritten part of the job description. One veteran coach's wife compared professional coaches to migrant workers, in that they never know where they will live from season to season. This makes it nearly impossible for a coach's wife to find and keep a job. Generally, if wives do work, it's usually as teachers or real estate agents or in other transferable professions.

For Lori Warhop, whose husband George is an assistant position coach, the transition between working and staying at home was a hard one. Until George's first NFL coaching job, Lori had worked outside the home. Of that time she said, "We were going along in our career paths side by side." But then Lori became pregnant with their first child, and like a lot of other coaching families, the couple decided that their children deserved a full-time mother, particularly since their father was going to be unavailable so much of the year. "Since he is gone so much, George and I . . . really try and make it so our kids feel a sense of security, to know that even though he's not there, I'm here."

Despite the couple's decision, like many moms, Lori missed the intellectual stimulation a workplace can provide, and having an absentee husband made her feel even more isolated. She says, "For me, that was the hardest time in our relationship. I was at home with a small baby that couldn't talk to me, and I needed someone to talk to, but George was never there."

Even if she wanted to return to the workforce, Lori knows that finding someone who would hire her would be extremely difficult. In years past, when Lori's jobs changed as often as her husband's college coaching positions, one potential employer told Lori that her resume read like she was "running from the law."

She describes a typical interview like this: "Employers would ask why I worked for only six months. I would tell them that my husband is a football coach. Sometimes it was beneficial and sometimes detrimental. Most of the people with whom I was interviewing were men, and they liked to talk about football. I could have a good, intelligent conversation about football, so that was the good part of my interview. "But, then it came down to the bottom line, 'How long are you going to be here, and why should I hire you?' I don't have a crystal ball. I cannot predict. All I could do is promise, 'While I'm employed by you, I will do a great job.'"

Player's wife Gina Nedney, who before she had a daughter worked as an occupational therapist, says, "Joe and I have moved around a lot, and the employer always asks me why I've moved to four different states. I've found it's just better to tell the truth. Once I told [prospective employers] that I would be leaving in August, and they said, 'We can't hire you to work just for four months.' But they recommended me to their registry, and that is how I got hired."

Gina says her football connection has "helped me in some ways because in one clinic in Arizona, the doctor was a big football fan and he knew of Joe. But it comes down to whether I'm a good therapist or not, and no one is going to hire me if I'm not qualified. Once they get to know me and more about my life, my employers don't focus on the football game."

Numerous veteran players' wives, especially those married to superstars, have said either publicly or informally that they are patiently waiting for the day their partners retire. Whether they plan on becoming business owners or rejoining a career where they left off, these women look forward to reentering the workforce. One famous player's wife explains, "He's worked so hard for so long. Let him have his time to rest and golf. Then it will be my turn to be out there, and he will be the one taking the kids to practice, volunteering, and doing homework."

"This Is Shannon—Her Husband's an NFL Coach"

My husband is not particularly well known. However, if someone is introducing me, his job always gets mentioned first, and quite often the person doing the introducing never gets around to talking about what I do at all. The talk immediately centers on the NFL, and that's usually where it stays. Wives of big-name players and popular head coaches have it fifty times worse than I do because for them the focus is always on their husbands. *Always.*

Jackie Rice has learned to take it in stride, but even if she is good humored about it, it still isn't easy. She says, "It is funny. You do have people who come up to us when Jerry and I are together. They will just wedge themselves between us to get closer to him or to take a picture. Sometimes people have a tendency to act like the wives don't exist. I was very fortunate to have a husband who never let people disrespect me in that way. He would say, 'You know, this is my wife Jackie.' He would always introduce me, or he would say, 'Excuse me, you just pushed my wife over,' or something like that. He would always make some reference so the person would acknowledge me."

Kim Singletary is right. Whether they like it or not, NFL women are defined by who their partners are and what they do for a living. The women become "football wives," and there is no escaping the label. Some women accept it with great pride, and others hide their association with the NFL as much as possible, for once this association is revealed, it becomes their primary identity, even with friends.

Throughout my husband's career, I've made a conscious attempt to distance myself from his job. I don't necessarily try to hide it, but I don't encourage people to talk to me about it either. For example, on Mondays, when my coworkers are attacking the intelligence of our offensive coordinator, whose wife I call a friend, I ignore their comments and bury myself in work. On Sunday morning, as numerous churchgoers stop me before the service to talk strategy and give me advice to "pass on" to my husband, I just politely smile and nod my head. When friends who are fans of a different team make it a point to e-mail me after a loss, playfully taunting me about our team's ruined chances for the playoffs, I lightheartedly laugh it off and try to talk some "smack" in return.

But the truth is, I care a great deal about my husband's job—and in ways that most people don't realize. No matter how much some of us might try to minimize it, the NFL plays a big role in all of our lives. We might wish that people would recognize us on our own terms once in a while, but we are also very emotionally involved in our partners' careers. When people criticize "my" team, it makes my blood boil, and after a win, I experience a deep sense of personal satisfaction. But it's not my job. It's not my defeat or victory.

If our husbands were dentists, lawyers, or contractors, I doubt we'd feel the same way. We would care about their work, but friends and strangers wouldn't make it a point to talk to us about every twist and turn. We wouldn't read about it in the newspapers and hear it on TV: "In dental news, veteran John Morton botched two fillings and ran late on another five appointments today. Rumors are flying that he's about to be replaced by a rookie dentist from Cleveland."

People outside of football place the game front and center in NFL women's lives, making it next to impossible for us not to become involved with our partners' careers. We may see through the hype, but we can't escape it. Professional football is an unusual profession. Its mystique is carefully packaged and sold, and many people are intrigued by it. Their curiosity is natural, and they want to talk and ask questions.

For instance, if a player is at an autograph signing but he is busy or not approachable, many sports fans will refer their sports-related questions to his wife or girlfriend. Actually, some people feel more comfortable and less intimidated asking the women NFL-related questions. From the veterinarian to the postal worker to the pediatrician to the gardener—everybody an NFL woman meets wants to talk football.

In the beginning, questions about their partners' careers are flattering. Women don't hesitate to tell others that their boyfriend or husband plays or coaches in the pros. It is exciting to be with someone who has, at least according to popular opinion, a fascinating and glamorous job. Attention and admiration are heaped onto NFL women simply because of their partners' famous jobs, and on their behalf, at least, they enjoy it.

"I am not bothered by it," one player's wife told me about fans approaching them when they're out together. "I enjoy it for him. He is doing something and working hard at it, and people recognize it. I like it when people talk to him and know his statistics and know things about him. I love that. And I am adamant about his taking the time to give people an autograph. I notice people before he does. I think it is important to give people time."

Kim Ruddy is more equivocal: "It depends. Sometimes I think

it's pretty neat. If we're sitting down with a mouthful of food and someone is running up to you, it's not very nice. I can't really say that I enjoy it, but it's nice that he has done well enough that people know who he is. I think it's nice for him in that respect."

However, after a couple of years—some women talked about arriving at this point sooner than others—NFL women take less pleasure in the hoopla. They no longer enjoy their partners' being recognized and drooled over in public. As one player's wife says, "He only plays football. He didn't hang the moon. Get off of him, please." Nor do women want to discuss their partners or the team in private either. When Rosemary Bennett hires house contractors, she gives them *her* name only. One linebacker's girlfriend says there is "less hassle involved and less explaining to do" if she limits what she says around strangers.

In the middle of a woman's fifth long season in the NFL, it's hard to listen to another woman exclaim, "Really, you are married to *him*? That is so cool! Your life must be so exciting!?" Nor is there any way to answer the men who ask in all seriousness, "Did your husband mention to you if the kick returner was out for the year?" Or "Why did the coach call that idiotic play?"

But fatigue is not the only reason women become more reticent about revealing their connections to the NFL as they get older. They discover that some people who respond with great friendliness at first have ulterior motives. In a week, are these people going to ask for free game tickets, merchandise, or an autograph? If they find out about the affiliation, are they going to "hate on" the team, the players, or the owner?

When Kori Shaw is asked what her husband does, she will go through three levels of progression. First, she says, "He works in town." If the next question is, "What does he do there?," Kori says, "Oh, he is a football coach." At this point Kori says people either "dismiss me for being married to a high school gym teacher, or their curiosity gets the better of them and they ask, "For what high school?" Level three is when Kori tells them that he coaches for the Ravens. "Then their eyes light up, and they say, 'Oh, *really*?' And it begins."

Some women have become suspicious of people wanting to be their friends simply to get close to their partners or to the

NFL. Several African American NFL women who live in gated, up-scale, mostly Caucasian areas said they were certain their neighbors would not be as welcoming if it were not for their husbands' employers.

As one woman said, "I just think they are a lot nicer to us. I think they would be a little more curious if they didn't know what he did. They're great people; I don't know how great they would be if we weren't football people."

After years of dealing with different situations, women can usually tell when people are genuine. Yet even close friends sometimes have a hard time seeing past the NFL's image. One player's wife says, "Some people I consider friends are still a little bit starstruck about the NFL. They might say, 'Oh, does Johnnie get to do this, and does he get to do that?' I wonder sometimes—even though I know they are good people and I trust them—I still wonder if there is an element . . . of being in awe of the situation. I don't think that is the reason they are friends with me, but I know that is a component of our relationship."

Pat Kennan also recognizes that this happens, but she says, "Sometimes the relationship just started out that way, but it opened a door to meeting someone new. So it didn't always have to be a negative thing because of an ulterior motive."

When Wives Suit Up

With the continual emphasis in public and in private on their partners, a few women sometimes lose themselves in pursuit of their partners' goals. These women become overly identified in their partners' celebrity, and they always use the plural "we" in reference to the job: "We signed a two-year contract." Or "We got fired from the Steelers." They also become very involved in their partners' workplace. They know who said what to whom, and they gossip about the players and coaches. According to one player's wife, some women "don't know where they stop and their husbands begin."

One example of this is when NFL women take on their husbands' problems, issues, or competition as their own. Surely every wife is protective of her husband—she cares for him, and if his job is in jeopardy, it is going to affect her. But some women will transfer a husband's personal conflicts with someone on the team onto that other person's wife. If one player takes over her husband's position, the wife will actively loathe that player's wife. Wives of coaches who are passed over for a promotion will immediately hold a grudge against the new coach's wife—before they have even met her! NFL wives tend to be very supportive of each other, and the main source of tension among them is usually this type of hurtful behavior.

Coach's wife Kathy Nolan, whose husband was a defensive coordinator during our interview, says, "I have been on staffs where there are women that just hate each other. It is the most awkward situation that you could ever imagine. Maybe someone was promoted over a particular woman's husband, and the husband came home and said, 'I can't stand this [newly promoted] guy.' Instead of separating herself from his job, the wife may pick up on that anger and put it on the other woman. That is not uncommon."

Kathy clearly sees this as a trap for all NFL women, even herself. "Not that my self-esteem is so strong and wonderful, but I have tried very hard to separate the women from the husbands. Obviously, not everyone gets along, but I think you can be not so connected. For example, Mike might have disagreed philosophically with another coach, or may even have been wronged by another coach, but I know that has nothing to do with his wife. Some other wives cannot separate that."

It has been said that wives' negative conduct can hurt their husbands' careers. One coach's wife confides, "The role of the NFL coach's wife is partially to play the game, do all the things you need to do, and be smooth about it. I've heard stories of women who fight with other wives, and then they get their husbands fired."

Still, most NFL women stop short of this sort of extreme identification and involvement. And as with a woman's self-confidence, one of the most important factors is the woman's husband. Several women stated that feeling valued by their partners made it easier for them to separate from the men's jobs. When NFL men recognize and respect the roles of wife, mother, and household manager (to name only a few), NFL women maintain a stronger sense of self. In their most important relationship, their marriage, NFL women come to know that they are more than a "football wife."

One woman said it is "definitely" difficult for NFL women to carve out their own personalities, but she added, "Fortunately, my husband gives me a lot of the recognition and support that I need in my life. If he didn't do that, it would be more difficult."

Kathy Nolan, who has no problems letting her husband know what is on her mind ("I don't mind arguing with Mike; I don't know if that is a blessing or a curse"), says that it took time for her and her husband to learn to appreciate the different but equally difficult challenges that an NFL life imposed on them. She says:

When we were young, we spent a lot of time competing about who has it worse. We got into this back-and-forth thing. You don't mean to be competitive, but you want it to be acknowledged how hard motherhood is. In his mind, he is thinking, "Well, don't you think it's hard for me? I can't see you. I can't see the baby." He won't verbalize that, but he will say, "Well, you try working with these guys."

Then I would end up being mad, thinking he has no idea. I would just love to leave him with the kids for three days. But now sometimes I sit there at a game and I think, I can't imagine having fourth and goal and if they score, we lose the game. How does he feel having to make that call? And now I think he looks at me when I am having to deal with the kids, and he thinks, "How does she do it?" I think we have really learned to respect and support each other.

6 Hello–Good-bye in the Not-For-Long League

One particular event often leaves a painful, angry scar over the hearts of NFL women: the cutting or firing of their husbands or boyfriends. Over time, NFL women may learn that being cut is just "part of the game," but regardless, most never forget—and in some cases refuse to forgive—the teams that give their partners the axe. Furthermore, no matter how many times it happens, a player's cut or a coach's firing never seems to get any less agonizing or traumatic for the women involved.

One wife to whom I spoke recalled the excitement she felt when her husband got his first coaching job on an NFL team. She bubbled with enthusiasm to everyone she met over their good fortune and the bright NFL future that awaited them—until the day one obviously disenchanted veteran coach's wife gave her an ominous warning: "Save all the money you can and hide the gun, because in a year or two he will be fired and then he will want to blow his head off."

The new-to-the-NFL wife says, "I was shocked. My stomach just dropped. I didn't know what to think. Was she serious? Is that the way the NFL really works?"

If there is one unwritten rule to life in today's NFL, it's that sooner or later nearly every player will be cut and almost every coach will be fired. And usually many times.

Sometimes the writing is in the sports pages. A team's season will be going down the toilet, and the swollen-knuckled fingers of blame will start pointing.

But more often, particularly for new players and coaches, being cut comes as a complete surprise. Up until the moment the player or coach is let go, the team seemingly couldn't be happier with his work. Teams fill their training camps with optimistic hopefuls because that's what they need, but the push of the season leads to many unfortunate players being shoved out the door.

The average career of an NFL player is 3.3 years. That's not the average length of time with one team; that's an entire career, start to abrupt finish. Some players spend twice as long in college as they will in the NFL, and they are likely to play for half a dozen teams in that time. Few players want to quit after three years, but that's how quickly most run out of options or energy.

As a consequence, NFL football bruises egos as forcefully and frequently as it does limbs, and if the player or coach in question is married and has a family, he isn't the only one feeling the pain. As we've seen, wives make huge sacrifices in their own lives to help their husbands pursue their NFL dreams, and wives become just as invested in the husbands' success. When their husbands fail—and they will, even through no fault of their own; that is just how the game is set up—NFL women experience the same trauma and anger the men do, perhaps even more so because an NFL woman can't do anything about it. She has no control over the situation. All she can do is watch and help pick up the pieces.

Do this once or twice, and you begin to wonder if a life in the NFL is even worth the price. Do this six, seven, a dozen or more times, and you may develop the same protective emotional callus as the veteran coach's wife quoted above.

The Wiser, the Warier

Like other women before a partner's first release, Gina Nedney assumed that when players made an NFL team, they would be there twelve to fifteen years. Now, however, when her friends ask if they can visit during the season, she tells them to wait until September to book their flights. She is not telling them to wait for better weather or a cheaper air fare; rather, Gina wants to ensure that her guests will actually have a place to stay.

At the time this book went to press, Gina's husband Joe, a place-kicker, was in year four of a five-year contract with the Tennessee Titans. Except for one period when he was placed on injured reserve with a torn ACL in his right knee, Joe's career has been thriving, and the couple, according to Gina, absolutely loves living in Nashville. But prior to his employment with the Titans, Joe was released from the Green Bay Packers, the Miami Dolphins, the Arizona Cardinals, the Oakland Raiders (twice), the Denver Broncos, and the North Carolina Panthers. That is a total of eight NFL moves in only six years.

Tucking a strand of dark brown hair behind an ear, Gina states, "I don't make any plans until he has made that final roster in September."

Gina's initiation into the NFL's transient ways came early. She says, "Our first year of marriage, Joe got released, and we didn't have anything in savings. He got beat out in camp. I think it was really hard on him. There was a lot of pressure on him to provide for us as a couple, because now we were married and he had moved me across the country. He was sad, upset, and mad, and I felt bad for him because he was upset. He actually made the team in Miami, but then he got cut the following year. I felt helpless and sad. It's out of my control, and there is nothing that I can do about it."

It has taken a while for Gina to accept that she has no control over these circumstances. When asked if her feelings of powerlessness put stress on her relationship, Gina answers, "It used to, but now I realize that just because he had a bad day it doesn't necessarily mean he is going to be cut. I try to let it pass. I also try to remember that I can't change yesterday, and tomorrow isn't here yet, so I try to deal with what is presented to me right now."

In the first few years of their marriage, which was also a time when Joe's career was particularly unstable, Gina says she thought her role was to be a cheerleader. She would always try to find something supportive and positive to say during the disappointing times. Now, however, she sees things differently: "I found that saying nothing at all and letting him talk is the best thing I can do for him. There is nothing I can say to change the situation, and there is nothing I can say to make him feel better because he knows what he did wrong if he had a bad game."

Gina says she's never considered not moving along with her husband to each new job and city. "My priority in my relationship is my husband. I don't know how other couples work, but we don't work when we are not together. The longest we've been apart since we were married is four weeks. When we're separated, I don't function well, and he doesn't function well. I don't see how it would work into a good situation."

One thing that Gina and other NFL women can control is how they handle their finances. Money, obviously, is always a top concern for NFL families during times of crisis. As we've seen, most NFL women don't work, so most typically don't have an income of their own to fall back on. Gina worked as an occupational therapist until the couple had their first child, but she has always watched the family finances carefully. She makes sure there is always emergency money in the bank, so when the next cut inevitably arrives, her family will not agonize over such things as losing a house to foreclosure or being forced to sell a car for cash.

"You could be getting this great payment one week, and the next week there won't be anything. Our friend played in the NFL; he was drafted and had all this money, and then he got released. For the last year and a half, he and his wife and their son have been living off their savings, trying to get back into the NFL. They are a perfect example of why you should not count your eggs until they're hatched. I'm very cautious and I'm very guarded."

Perhaps remarkably, Gina speaks without bitterness or cynicism about all the life-altering upheaval they've had to endure. Instead, she thinks it's had a positive influence, and many NFL women say the same thing.

After Joe was cut the first time, when they were still newlyweds, Gina says, "He depended on me for my income. I supported us for the first couple of months until he got a job with another team. I think he realized how important teamwork is. It forced us to depend on each other. This lifestyle can make you stronger as a couple. In our experience, getting cut has brought us closer, especially because we are not around family. I think it is a good thing that has happened to us."

Running Laps

During the 1999 playoff season, the public could not get enough of the media's dramatic account of the rise-to-the-top Cinderella story of Super Bowl MVP Kurt Warner. Segment upon segment aired depicting Warner's pre-superstar days, which were spent bagging groceries for minimum wage, eating meals purchased with food stamps, and living in his girlfriend's parents' basement. At long last, many longtime NFL people sighed, football fans were finally getting a glimpse into the harsh and dismal experience of an NFL dreamer.

In one significant way, however, the multitude of rags-to-riches commentaries still misled the public. They presented Kurt and Brenda Warner's hard times, lack of money, and suffering—all while trying to make an NFL roster—as extraordinary, when in fact Warner's past is typical of thousands of players striving to "make it" in the NFL. And most of these players will not remain in the league long enough to dull the tips of their cleats, let alone become Super Bowl MVPs.

This side of professional football is rarely discussed. Given the intense scrutiny the sport receives in the media and from the public, this may or may not be surprising. Nearly all the attention is focused on the illustrious, charmed careers of a few, while the efforts of the vast multitude are hardly mentioned.

The road to the NFL properly begins in college. Players can certainly get the attention of pro scouts in high school, but it's in college that they start to refine their raw talents and prove what they might be able to do at the professional level. For some players, all of college is one long audition for the NFL, but the real thing is the NFL Combines.

After being rated by a committee, all draft-eligible, pre-qualified college players are invited to the NFL Combines, which are held in mid-February in Indianapolis. Usually just over three hundred college players get pre-qualified and attend this NFL "audition." After enduring a full slate of physical drills and testing—which includes the 40-yard dash, agility tests, 60-yard shuttle, broad jump, vertical jump, and various drills for individual positions—players are required to conduct interviews with NFL coaches. Doctors and medical experts spend a lot of time combing the athletes' bodies for weak spots and injuries so a team knows exactly in what areas its investment might be lacking or deficient.

M. J. Duberstein of the NFLPA research department believes it is just as important for these young athletes to strut their mental muscles. He says, "How a football player reacts under pressure and stress at The Combine is becoming just as important as his physical attributes. Maturity, poise, and the ability to fight through adversity are critical at the professional level."

Every player's goal is to impress the various team personnel, scouts, and coaches in hopes of being drafted at the end of April. An impressive Combine workout from a player from a smaller school could increase his status on draft day.

In the weeks before his Combine performance, a player is likely to sign with an agent. If the agent is the type who extends loans, this may be the first time the young player has ever had any significant money. The closer it gets to draft time, the more media attention and hype the player receives.

If the player isn't drafted, then he automatically becomes a free agent. Free agents are eligible to speak to and negotiate with any teams. It is typically the player's agent's job to sign him to a contract with a team. In either case—whether a player is drafted or is a free agent—if he and the team agree on the terms of a contract, the player will attend training camp in July. Only players under contract are allowed to attend training camp, but these players need to make the team before the terms of their contract kick in—and there is no guarantee that a player will make the team. According to M. J. Duberstein, less than half (only 44 percent) of first-year players going to training camp will make the final active roster of fifty-three players. Finally, if a drafted player is cut in training camp, he automatically becomes a free agent.

While it doesn't seem like there'd be any functional difference between being a rookie free agent or a draft pick at training camp, that isn't so, according to longtime player agent Bill Heck: "There is an upward battle being a free agent. There is no question about it. You are not going to get the reps, and you are not going to get the chance that the other guys will get to impress. If free agents can get into a pre-season game and get on film—and do some things like score a touchdown or catch a long pass or maybe run it back for a touchdown—those things will catch a team's eye and get them noticed."

Plainly put, at summer training camp teams need bodies. They need hungry, "give it 'til you don't got no more" rookies. Some scouts, general managers, and personnel people will say anything to get a player's signature on a contract. For proof, consider the fact that teams bring an average of eighty players into camp, while the final roster is whittled down to fifty-three, with eight guys on the practice squad. This means one out of four players will be cut before the season even starts.

Regardless, players hear comments all the time like, "A guy with your type of speed can make this team complete." Or "You need to work on a few things, but your chances here are excellent." Sure, personnel people hope that the no-name greenie will turn out to be the next Jerry Rice. But if not, the team has enough extra "legs" to run a decent scout team against the veterans.

Teams can afford to do this because despite the contracts, younger players with less than four accrued seasons on an NFL roster can be cut at any time, be it before or during the season, and teams never have to pay them another dime. Furthermore, players with four years or more of service have their salary guaranteed only if they are on the roster at the time of the first game. Thus a good number of veterans are released at the final cut and then signed back after the first game. This way teams can pay players from week to week as they need them. Considering this—along with the fact that the average player's career is less than four years—it's easy to see how teams work the system to their financial advantage.

Player agent Bill Heck says, "There is a small percentage of players in the NFL who have their position made on the team every year, but most players have no security. Ability from the thirtieth guy on the team down to the fifty-third guy on the team is very similar. I would say the majority of players that come out, including the draft picks and the rookie free agents, will run the 'NFL lap' at least one time."

Running an NFL lap typically means going through training camps with two or three teams, going through two or three off-season workout programs, and maybe even playing in Europe. Players do not make a lot of money during all these efforts, and a few years of them can really wear players down, especially if they are not single. Indeed, an NFL hopeful and his significant other can quickly get tired of running laps and waiting for their rags-to-riches segment to air.

The Coaches' Shuffle

NFL owners are not known for their patience and understanding during a losing streak. They want someone, somewhere, held accountable, whether that person is the main culprit or not. It could be that the team has a bunch of seasoned but mediocre veteran players, but it would be impossible to get rid of them because of the huge hit in the salary cap. So instead, the head coach gets sacked.

In this increasingly high-pressure, win-driven NFL world, the firing of head coaches has become as predictable as punting on fourth and twenty. According to Larry Kennan, the executive director of the NFLCA, NFL coaches get fired, hired, and relocated on average every nineteen months. Kennan says the rationale of teams who fire their head coach is always the same: "At the end of the day, when owners hire a new coach, it is either because the new coach is a tougher disciplinarian or he is a better communicator or whatever. Whatever the other guy wasn't, that is what the new guy is."

Usually, most assistants on staff are dismissed with their leader. At other times, assistant position coaches are retained until a new head coach is hired. These coaches are usually given a chance to interview with the new head coach—unless he has already assembled his staff, which is usually made up of coworkers or friends from past teams. In that case, the redundant assistants are then terminated.

One example of the assistant coaches' lack of control over their jobs is that when a head coach is fired, sometimes his assistants are denied permission to seek employment with other teams, even though they have no guarantees or promises that they will be retained. Larry Kennan considers that these in-limbo coaches are being held "hostage."

Eventually, every fired coach will look to interview for vacancies at other teams, either in the pros or college. But sometimes positions elsewhere are filled, and the fired coach has no choice but to sit out the balance of the season and attempt to be hired the following year.

A very few assistant coaches get fired while they are still under contract, and those who are continue to receive their salaries for the year (though they sometimes have to fight for this). However, all job benefits end: health insurance, 401K contributions, pension contributions, and car allowances. For the vast majority of assistant coaches who are not under contract, being fired means no more salary as well. For the predominance of NFL couples who have only one working spouse—the husband—this means no income until the husband is employed again, and this could be anywhere from two days to six months to never—at least not in the NFL.

One coach's wife says, "We are the worker ants. We are the expendables—even though we are the motor, and without us you can't go forward. But owners think, Oh, we can get rid of them and bring in other worker ants, and they can do just as well. It is a dichotomy. It is all a part of the crazy business we are in."

Another coach's wife now sees the first firing almost as a right of passage. While she says you "get really hurt," she maintains the following:

> You are not a real coach until you have been fired. You have to learn how to be resilient in this business, and you have to learn how to promote yourself, and you have to know how to network. All those things are important in being a professional coach. It is a good old boys' society of who knows whom.
>
> Until you've been fired, how do you know how this works? You get the first job because you knew somebody. They thought you were a good kid, so they brought you along. Then you get fired, and you find out: Well, do I know enough people in this business? Do I have a network? And the people that I know, do they know anybody? Then you start making your phone calls. You start building your little base, and then it just grows from there. Until you have been fired, you don't really know how this thing works.

Every Cut Runs Deep

Experiencing the pain of an NFL cut or firing even once changes an NFL woman forever. The first time it happens, a woman is usually stunned. Any information she receives about her partner's performance comes from the partner. Out of denial or fear, some players don't communicate the possibility of their getting cut to their wives or girlfriends. A team's win/loss record is usually a good indication of an eminent coach's firing, but not always.

Other times, players and coaches are blown away when they hear their job has been terminated, and a cut or firing is always effective immediately. There is no "two-week notice." Some coaches are let go mere hours after stepping off the field for the last game of the season. By the time a player turns in his playbook, signs a release form, cleans out his locker, and takes his post-physical exam, he is often too overcome with bitterness, sorrow, or both to think clearly. Left with only his turf shoes as souvenirs, he is unable to explain to his wife or girlfriend why it happened and, more important, what will happen next. This reaction, or lack thereof, only increases a woman's confusion and anxiety.

Pat Kennan recalls, "The first time, it was with the Raiders. It was a phone call, and we were just told that the head coach had resigned and that we were free to look for jobs elsewhere. It was a real sick feeling. There were only four other openings in the NFL that year. It just makes you feel sick to your stomach. I've got friends now, and I just say, I know the feeling. It is a horrible feeling."

Pat says that the horrible feeling continues "until they get the next job. When they get the next job, then it is okay." But she adds, "You're going to have to move, and you're going to have to sell your house, and you have got to uproot your kids. No, it never got easier. I never got used to it, and I don't think my husband did either."

For me, the second time my boyfriend was cut was far worse than the first. John had an inkling he'd get released from his first training camp with the Raiders, but during his second one with the Packers, he was getting nothing but positive feedback. Plus, I'd left college to join him in Green Bay, completely committing *my* life to his situation as well. When he was cut, my anger at the deception of John's coaches and my panic over suddenly being unable to control my life were more intense than anything I'd ever felt. I have a lasting memory of blurting out irrationally, but in all seriousness, "We are going to have to move. We will probably have to join the army!"

I eventually calmed down and my practical side kicked in, but nothing was the same for me after the Packer cut. The attraction and the allure I felt upon seeing the red, white, and blue NFL insignia—gone. The excitement I experienced sitting beside John as he signed yet another contract—and there were many in his five-year "playing" career—no more. To this day, I feel a sense of dread on August 30, which is typically the last day of training camp cuts. My NFL motto became, "Don't trust them. Don't believe them. Don't get your hopes up." If John wanted to continue pursuing his dream, fine, but I knew that I could never put my heart and hopes into the NFL again. I renewed my softball career and focused on graduating from college.

Other women to whom I spoke react just as strongly, if not more so. A tight end's wife said she would have spit on the doctor of the team that released her husband based on the doctor's medical recommendation. She says, "I was pissed. It wasn't right because he was working his ass off to get healthy." The player went on to find success with another team, but his wife's vendetta did not diminish. "I always want that team to lose, and lose badly."

The intensity of these reactions has to do with the stakes that are involved, sometimes the simple stress that comes from being fired from any job, and sometimes the high-profile nature of the situation. Perhaps a player's wife knows she will have to spend weeks or months comforting her distraught child once he discovers his family will be moving thousands of miles from his best friend. Or possibly a coach's wife opened her door one morning during a losing season only to find a "For Sale" sign mercilessly staked in her yard. Unbelievable as it may seem, more than one coach's wife described this happening to her. Maybe the coach has become so despondent over his firing that his wife believes he may become suicidal.

Most people would consider being fired even once as one of the most traumatic experiences in their professional careers. Along with a family death and relocating, being fired is general recognized as one of life's three most stressful events. In the NFL, it can happen every year, and the whole world knows about it.

Losing an NFL job is exponentially more traumatic because of the public nature of the dismissal. Sports pages carry daily signings and releases in the "transactions" box. And, of course, thanks to the Internet, anyone can log onto a football web site and read about a player's or coach's "failure" mere minutes after it has taken place.

After one coach's particularly brutal firing (his players had continually bad-mouthed him to the media), his wife admitted that her husband used alcohol to escape. "I couldn't get him off the couch for weeks. Finally, he came around after I threatened to leave. Until he found another job, it was a devastating time for the whole family."

Oftentimes the players and coaches themselves are at a loss to understand why they were let go. Explaining it to inquiring family and friends can be next to impossible, and not everyone has the player's or coach's feelings uppermost in mind.

One player's girlfriend remembered that he received a call from his aunt and uncle the day after he was released from training camp. "Why didn't the coach like you?" they probed their nephew. "Aren't you good enough?" In some cases, family members have become dependent on their son's, brother's, or cousin's income, and this only adds to the pressure and stress of a cut or firing.

One wife says, "We helped both of our siblings out with a down payment on a car. We told them his contract wasn't guaranteed, and we had put enough down on the cars to where the payments were low enough that if they had to take them over, then they could, and they were completely understanding about that. But I think that was a concern of theirs when he was released: 'Oh crap, what about this now? How long is he going to be out?' "

No Guarantees
Let it be known that my husband John is the first to admit that he did not have NFL-level receiver skills. Looking at past playing film of himself, John is unforgiving in his critique: "I wasn't good enough to make it in this league. Plain and simple."

That's fine for John to say, but he wasn't *untalented*. If he lacked certain skills or technique that kept him from being regarded as "the best" when he played for Western Michigan University, John still possessed something that could never be taught or improved upon by repetition. He was fast. At the NFL Combines, he ran a 4.36, and he was so quick that some of his teammates affectionately nicknamed him "White Lightning."

It was in large part because of his speed that some football analysts thought John might be drafted out of college, possibly in a middle round. He wasn't drafted, and thus he began what would turn out to be five years of running laps around the league as a free agent. But teams never discouraged him with a mountain of negative statistics and the low probability of success. No, they encouraged him—constantly. It's doubtful that my ultra-positive husband would have listened if anyone had tried to discourage him, but no one did. Perhaps if *I'd* known that the average NFL career is just over three years, I would have felt differently when teams cut John loose. Maybe I would have rationalized, "Oh well, those are the averages. That's the way things are in the NFL." But I doubt that, too.

Nobody feeds you dismal statistics when you're a young player trying to make it in the NFL. Instead, they pump you up. Perhaps it was my Midwest naiveté, but I never understood how teams could lie, or at the very least change their minds so quickly about players. Now that John is on the other side of the ball, however, I have a better understanding of how and why teams sign the lower-rung, nondrafted players.

Like John, many players pass through who are never quite good enough, but the NFL needs cheap bodies who will work hard for a promise, and so they are encouraged to stick it out. Others never make it because of money or politics. Some players make the roster, but after a season or two they get cut in favor of someone younger, faster, and cheaper. Teams will sometimes keep a less deserving veteran because his name continues to sell jerseys. Then, of course, there is plain old luck. Being in the right place at the right time can play a big role in who gets his name on the back of a jersey—for example, making a crucial catch during a pre-season game or being available when an injury to another player creates an opening on the roster.

No matter what team representatives say, there are *no* guarantees that players will make the squad. As one player's wife aptly puts it, "I realize now, these people are not out to protect his well-being.

You have got to be prepared, no matter if you're on the top or the bottom. Anything always can happen."

Moving On

Within the first week or two of a firing, many NFL women become optimistic again. They believe in their partners and trust that they will get picked up by another team. As Kathy Waufle says about coaches, "It's like one big family, and if you haven't burned any bridges, things should work out fine. As long as you're a hard worker and a great coach, I don't think there is anything to worry about."

In the hours, days, and weeks following an NFL firing, the telephone rings incessantly. In addition to the calls from family and friends, players phone their agents in the hope that they have scheduled a tryout with another team. An agent contacts numerous teams to determine their needs, and then he calls the player with updates. Terminated assistant coaches dial in to an unofficial "coaching hotline," where they speak with other coaches to find the buzz on possible openings.

This telethon never shuts down. After a defensive coach was diagnosed with cancer midway through a season, there were, his wife says, "at least four or five guys calling around trying to find out what they were going to do with his job." Years later, she remains incredulous: "I mean, the guy is fighting cancer, and others are calling trying to get his job."

It takes just one firing for NFL women to become experts at buying and selling houses, relocating their children to different schools, and finding new doctors—all, needless to say, unassisted by their husbands. When a player or coach begins a new job, he leaves almost immediately, while his wife or girlfriend is left behind to tie up loose ends.

Gina Nedney designates herself as "the moving company. If he is there, he helps me move to our next location. But if it's training camp or midseason and he is not around, it's up to me."

The NFL women didn't even mention carrying seventy-pound boxes up two flights of stairs and traipsing through unfamiliar streets in search of a twenty-four-hour pharmacy among the hassles of moving. The main concern was the effect that frequent moves had on children. One coach was fired just weeks after he and his family finished building a custom-made house. Then he got another job in New Orleans, and his wife moved their family 2,500 miles to a new home. They lived there seven months—until the coach was fired again. She says, "My poor kids had moved four times in three years at that point."

As we'll see in chapter 7, this is just one of the tough aspects of NFL life to which kids must adjust.

Pulling Back

Everyone knows moving is hard work, and, as mentioned, relocating is among the top three of life's most stressful events. What's more, it takes a lot of time and energy—no matter how outgoing one is—to immerse oneself in a new community. It is emotionally draining for NFL women to make these investments over and over, only to be ripped away again when their partners get cut or fired. It is so draining, in fact, that some NFL women stop making the effort. They either refuse to relocate and so live separately from their partners, or they make the move but withdraw socially.

The girlfriend of a running back says, "I got to the point where I put up walls and thought, 'Why should I get involved?' Things will just change again. It's too much work. Why should I put myself through all this just to do it all over again? For what and for who? I had a very terrible attitude."

Gina Nedney says the efforts she makes socially depend on the nature of her husband's situation: "A few years ago, we were with the Panthers. Joe signed six weeks into the season, and he was only there to replace the injured kicker. We knew we weren't going to stay the following year, so I didn't get involved in the community. I got to know the punter and his wife, and that was all. But when we signed a five-year deal with the Titans the following year, I joined a swim team at the YMCA, and I went to the Titans' wives' Bible study group to meet and worship with other wives."

Gina also stated that although she has received a lot of support from other NFL wives—who will offer helpful advice and other pointers to new-to-town women—the transitory lifestyle of some players prevents couples from getting close to others. "I think the longer some people are at a team, the more friends they make, and the more social they are. If you have a lot of transition with a lot of players coming in and out, it is hard to form that bond, and some wives are a little reluctant to get together."

It is unusual, however, for wives in the coaching circles to pull back from one another. They tend to have a deep personal connection. They are the only people who truly understand and can empathize with "the life." When one coach is fired, it is not uncommon for another coach's wife to invite his wife and children into her home until the coach finds another job. Though not necessarily best friends, coaches' wives share a strong bond because their husbands are doing the same thing—holding on until they get fired or until something better comes along. Even if one team's staff breaks up, the NFL coaching circle is small enough that wives know they will likely meet again at another team in the future.

This same closeness does not exist between players' wives and coaches' wives. On the part of coaches' wives, there is some disdain for the other side because, according to a veteran coach's wife, "the players' wives' lives are so different." This has everything to do with the different levels of income and the disparate number of hours that veteran players and coaches spend at work. As for players' wives, they stated they did not become overly friendly with coaches' wives because they didn't want to be perceived as "kissing up" to the boss's wife.

One player's wife says, "Who wants to hang out with your boss? It would just be a little awkward. Nothing personal, but this is still a business."

Another player's wife says, "We started a wives' Bible study, and we discussed if we should have the coaches' wives involved or not. Do you want to go there with your group of friends or people you are in the same circle with? What if your husband is having a problem with a coach? You just don't know about the confidentiality. It's not like the two groups don't like each other. I think it's a different age group, too. Most of the coaches' wives are older, and their kids are older, and they are doing different things. There is that, and there is also just the dynamic. It's not only a boss. It's more than a boss."

Perhaps the main reason for distance between the two groups goes back to the ugly aftermath of NFL firings. For the two groups to be friends, there needs to be a careful understanding and distinction between their friendship and their husbands' professional relationships.

As one coach's wife explains, "I'm careful about getting too close with players' wives. I don't want them turning around and blaming my husband, and therefore me, for what happens to their husbands. If you are best friends with your husband's player's wife and he gets cut, it might get messy."

What Didn't Kill Us . . .

Looking back at John's playing days, I am grateful that my negativity over the cuts never discouraged John. More than once, with his jaw locked in determination, John confided, "I can feel it this time, Shan. This time they are gonna keep me." Sadly, it never happened. To his credit, however, throughout all the cuts and pickups, the releases and re-signings, John's work ethic remained impeccable. Without questions or complaints, he did whatever his coaches and the personnel asked of him. John lived by the powerful words tattooed on his right calf: "Intensity, Determination, and Discipline."

Yet after five tumultuous (but exciting) years, the slogan "Have gym bag, will travel" (as my mother used to say) was getting worn. Though it had happened to me years before, the extreme highs and lows of football had finally taken their toll on John. He wasn't having fun anymore. He was tired and weary. Plus, five years of living apart—sometimes in different countries—was a lot for a young couple to endure. It was impossible for us to make plans for the future. Our fate always seemed to rest in the hands of one team or another; it was always contingent on a team's needs and wants.

The decision came while John and I sat on the edge of a small double bed in a hotel room in Frankfurt, Germany, at the end of his one season in the NFL's World League. For two hours, I quietly held my best friend's hand as he painfully deliberated shelving his dream, the one dream, the NFL. John asked me, "Would it be giving up? You know I'm not a quitter, right? I just don't know if I can go through another camp again."

Following our intense heart-to-heart, John talked with his agent, after which he turned down an offer to attend yet another training camp, this time with the Forty-Niners. Instead, he made an international phone call to the Oakland Raiders. Unlike with so many others, John's sweat, blood, and tears was not shed on the professional field in vain. The lanky wide receiver's character and positive attitude had been recognized by the Oakland Raiders' principle owner, Al Davis.

Mr. Davis offered John an internship in the scouting department at $150 a week—the usual position and pay for everyone who has a start in Raider Nation. Several months later, Jon Gruden was named head coach of the Raiders. Remembering the ambitious, hard-working Green Bay wideout, Gruden knew that John's personality—single-minded, workaholic, and driven—would make for a great coach. Gruden had an opening on his coaching staff for an offensive assistant.

Having heard stories about the tremendously long hours coaches worked, John and I were both ambivalent. After talking it over, we agreed that he should try it for one season, and then we would reevaluate. Although now an observer, standing apart from the physical action, John was thrilled to be back in the game. After just one season, he was bitten by the coaching bug. I knew then there was nothing anyone could say that would make him turn back.

Experiencing the pain of the uglier side of professional football bent us, for sure, but we never broke. The trials and tribulations of the last twelve years have made us turn to each other for support. In the end, the Not-For-Long League has made us stronger, both as a couple and as individuals.

7 Raising Football Kids

Growing up is hard enough without the added problems NFL life can bring. For any youngster, dealing with an absentee father, switching schools, coping with jealousy and ridicule from other kids, and handling the pressure to be "just like Dad" present difficult challenges. All these things are heightened by a life in the NFL; in addition, children have to deal with a parent in a high-profile profession who is himself sometimes a celebrity.

Bringing kids up right in this challenging environment is a number one priority for NFL families, and this is another reason some NFL women choose not to work outside the home. Particularly in coaches' households, during the season Mom will be the primary caregiver—in fact, nearly a single parent. NFL women who have, or plan to have, children, often ask themselves what's more important, their careers or raising their children. It's a simple decision.

In terms of family, players and coaches are often in very different situations. Most players are young, and their careers are relatively short—even the most successful rarely last more than a decade—so most are out of the league before their kids hit adolescence. In contrast, coaches tend to be older by the time they get to the NFL, and their pro careers are longer. In a coach's household, it's not unusual for children to spend their entire upbringing inside football.

Most NFL families also face a further level of difficulty. Their children are being raised in households, and in lifestyles, that are usually dramatically different than the ones in which their parents grew up. At the same time that NFL parents themselves are learning to cope with unfamiliar issues of fame and wealth, they have to somehow teach their children how to negotiate them. Every parent wants to raise self-assured, poised children with a healthy, balanced perspective on life, but for football kids, the sometimes strange, unusual world of the NFL is the only world they know.

My Three Sons

Pat and Larry Kennan have three sons, all of them now grown and on their own, and all born and raised while their father was a football coach. For thirteen years, Larry worked as an offensive coach in college football; then in 1982 he jumped to the pros, where he started as the quarterback coach for the Oakland Raiders. Larry spent sixteen years in the NFL, eventually becoming an offensive coordinator, and he worked for seven different NFL teams (for the Raiders twice). In 1997, after a bad experience with the New England Patriots (the team tried to break his contract), Larry decided to take a year off from coaching. During that time he was asked by other professional coaches to help them organize. Larry never put on another coach's headset; instead, on February 1, 1999, Larry was named the executive director of the NFLCA (described in chapter 3). He remains in that position today.

Always stylishly dressed, fun-loving, and bubbly, Pat Kennan is a small-town girl from California—who signs every e-mail with "love and light, Pat"—and she was always among the most well liked of the coaches' wives throughout the league. Even though her status has changed, she is just as well liked today. When asked to describe herself, Pat answers, "Resilient." Bringing up three boys in the unstable, highly mobile NFL has definitely helped make her that way, especially since she has done so much of the parenting solo.

Her husband was in attendance for the birth of each of their children, but there have been close calls. After their first child was born in November, Pat said she would never have another child during football season. Mother Nature, however, makes her own plans, and sure enough their second and third sons were also fall babies. Larry's team was in town when his second child was born, so getting to the hospital wasn't a problem, but for the third child, Larry was on the road. Luckily, someone tracked him down with news that his wife was about to give birth, and he made it to Pat's side with an hour to spare. Pat laughs when she says, "I thought I wouldn't have any of them during football season, and I had all of them then."

Moving has been one of the big issues for the Kennans while raising kids. Perhaps one of Pat's most memorable moves occurred early in her husband's career, when Larry became the offensive coordinator at the University of Nevada at Las Vegas. Pat recalls:

I had a two-year-old, and my second baby was two months old. We moved into a hotel. The moving truck driver had all of our belongings, and he said that he would be following me and arriving shortly after me.

The hotel was not family friendly. It didn't even have high chairs for the baby. It was really hard, so I decided that it would be easier to go sleep on the floor of our new townhouse that night and take care of the babies there rather than try and keep them in a hotel. Of course, Larry was gone recruiting.

Well, the truck didn't show up. It took five days to get there! So I was sleeping on the floor of the townhouse for five nights with two babies, not knowing anybody in town. What happened was the company couldn't find the truck because the truck driver was holed up on the other side of town with his girlfriend.

When they finally located the truck, changed drivers, and delivered my stuff, it was like 6 p.m., and it started raining—and it never rains in the desert! I was trying to check off the driver, feed a hungry baby, and get everything indoors as quickly as possible. I'll never forget those five days.

Pat sighs, laughing.

Moving a houseful of children never became easier, but looking back, Pat says that constantly encountering new experiences and new places had a positive effect on her sons' personalities. Pat says,

"My kids are very comfortable with all types of people. They are very adaptable, and they are very outgoing. Plus, being a coach's sons opened doors for them. Their friends thought of them as special, especially because my boys all played sports."

Pat speculates that perhaps moving and adapting to new places and schools is easier for boys than for girls. She says, "I don't think boys tend to be as cliquey, so when they move, it is easier for them to become friends and be part of the in-group. I think that girls are a little more cliquey than boys. Maybe it is different today because girls' sports are bigger, and maybe there are other things they can get involved in, but it seems like for my friends who had daughters, it was a little bit harder for the girls. Maybe girls just express their emotions more."

All three boys enjoyed their father's connection to the NFL. They all played sports and followed the NFL closely, and they were thrilled every time they got the chance to meet famous professional athletes. Pat clearly remembers the first time, the year that Larry became the quarterback coach for the Oakland Raiders: "We came out to visit and find a place to live. We were sitting in a coffee shop, and Gene Upshaw came over to the table. He was really nice to the kids. He was the first pro player that my kids ever met. They asked him to flex his muscles. And he did."

Pat remembers another memorable encounter: "You know Howie Long, how he wears his hair in a flat top? Well, my middle son was at training camp in the summer, and he told his dad, 'I like Howie's hair cut like that so much, I'm getting my hair cut like that, too.' And he's been wearing his hair like that ever since."

A coach's long hours and the dedication his job requires put a special burden on children, but Pat feels that it's had a positive influence in their home. "I think that my husband is so special that I don't think it did affect them negatively. We all understood that when we could be number one, we were. We just knew that he loved all of us. We were all very loved. We knew that that was just the nature of his job."

Of course, that didn't mean that taking care of three boys basically by herself during the season was easy. Pat preferred the off-season because Larry was around more to help with the kids. But, she says, the off-season carried its own difficult adjustment. "The roles change," she says simply, laughing. "During the season I was in charge; then all of a sudden I'm the VP. Throughout the years, I am sure it got better just because I knew it was coming."

Unlike the children of players, coaches' kids don't really experience much external pressure to grow up to be "just like Dad," but they do experience criticism and/or jealousy from their peers because of what their fathers do. Pat says her boys experienced all sorts of negative reactions and harsh teasing from their friends, and they expressed their own anger in a number of ways, some amusing. "I remember them telling me the kids at school would say, 'Boy, your dad's team got beat bad,' and they would say, 'Well, your dad's team didn't play at all.' Or they might say, 'Don't look at me; I'm not to blame. I'm not a coach.' They learned to deal with it."

Smiling, Pat says, "I'll tell you a funny story. When my husband was fired from the Seahawks, our son went up to basketball practice. When he came home, he said, 'Mom, I almost got in a fight with this kid. [The kid] asked me where my truck was. He said, 'I thought that maybe you had to sell it because your dad got fired.'"

Pat continues, "I said, 'You know why he said that, don't you?' I was going to say because he was probably jealous. He said, 'Yeah, because he is a dickhead, Mom.'"

In the moment, Pat had to stifle her own laughter. "I said, 'Yeah, you're right, that too.'"

Pat says, "When we were in Indianapolis, Larry got fired. The same son was in his bedroom; he had a picture of the head coach, and he was throwing darts at it. The whole family just broke up laughing."

How are the boys doing today? Pat says, "Our three sons are all grown. The oldest got married in July and lives in Indianapolis. Our middle son coaches at North Stafford High School, near where we live [in Virginia]. It is rated number one right now of the state's number five and number six division schools. We enjoy going to his games. Our youngest son works for the NFLCA. His dad finds his help invaluable, because he knows most of the coaches and understands the coaching life and challenges firsthand."

The Coach, the Kid, and the Single Mom

During the season, in every NFL family, the wife becomes primarily responsible for raising the children. In a coach's household, the wife is almost 100 percent responsible for their physical, educational, and emotional well-being. Children of coaches might see their fathers only one to three hours a week during the football season. Players' kids are a bit luckier. While they don't get to see their dads much when the team starts training camp or during the eight weekends of the season when the team has away games, most nights during the season players are home for dinner. Plus, players have Tuesdays off.

As expected, according to the majority of coaches' wives, the most difficult part of raising children is doing it alone. From the beginning of camp in mid-July to the end of the season, sometime in January, they are basically single mothers. NFL families also rarely live near their extended families, so wives do not get much outside help either. Like similar absentee-father/mother-only households, nearly every "family" event is spearheaded and carried out by the woman. However, the primary advantage in an NFL household—and it is significant—is that there is no financial pressure for the woman to work outside the home.

Gay Nell Shaw, the wife of veteran defensive coach Willie Shaw and the mother of three grown children, reflects:

> When the kids were between birth and five, I lost my ability to have an adult conversation. I have three children, so my life revolved around caring for their needs, being the domestic diva, writing bills, getting the house cleaned, and being a wife when I saw my husband. When my husband would come home, I was excited to sit down and have an adult conversation, and he would be pooped. It was a time that I felt alone and asked myself, When does somebody take care of me? That was the difficult part—not having a pity party, but learning to etch out the time where I could have an adult time with my husband or with other women.

Many coaches' wives go to great lengths to make up for their partners' parenting slack. These Supermom's do it all, whether it's taking care of all the Christmas shopping and decorating, coaching Little League, snapping photos of Junior's prom, or lugging furniture to the freshman dormitory. It is both ironic and sad that an NFL coach rarely attends his own kids' football games. Usually, the wife will videotape a child's game, and the coach will watch it later, at work, if he has time.

One coach's wife says, "I know I don't schedule the kids for as much stuff as they would like to be involved in because there is no possible way I can drive one to a 7:30 Boy Scouts' meeting when the other one has to be in bed by 8 or 8:30. But if my husband was home at 6, I could schedule the activities knowing that he would be home or could help out with the driving too."

As much as possible, these hardworking moms try to connect their children with their fathers. Some mothers will alter their babies' sleeping schedules during the season to match their fathers' working schedules—even for a twenty-minute visit. Other mothers will sit their children in front of the television, cajoling them, "Come on, honey, it's time to see your daddy." For coaches' kids, these glimpses of the sidelines might be the biggest chunk of time they see their fathers all week.

During the season at least, wives and children of coaches conduct the majority of their relationship on the telephone. One coach's wife describes their family's bedtime routine: "Every night at 9 p.m., we have our secret code, where Daddy knows it is us calling. The kids always want to say good night to him. He asks them about their day at school and the tests they had. Most of their conversations are on the phone. He is always working when we are talking, but he still has an ear open for the important things."

For coaches' kids, this limited time spent with their fathers is sometimes all they know, so complaints are rare. Still, there are many NFL coaches who feel terrible about the huge chunks of time they spend away from their families. These fathers, when they are home, don't waste a moment. They would never space out in front of the sports channel while their kids shoot hoops alone. Even while at work, these fathers attempt to stay as involved as possible. They phone their kids every day, sometimes numerous times a day, to talk with them and reassure them that if he could, Dad would be with them, cheering at their track meet or watching their theatre production.

Not all fathers are like this, of course, and there are several reasons why NFL dads willingly cede parenting to their wives. Even though players are physically home much more often than their coaches, the stress of playing in the NFL means that they are not always fully present when they *are* home. Likewise, some coaches become obsessed with finding "the key" to the next win, and even when they have a rare Friday evening or Saturday afternoon off, they fixate on football.

One coach's wife described the following scene one night at the dinner table: "The whole time we were eating, he was taking notes and doing all these charts. One daughter was trying to tell him something, and he got really upset. He told her she didn't understand. He said, 'Nothing is as important as making it to the Super Bowl.' Both the girls got really upset with that because it's not the most important thing. In his eyes, it is, but your kids are going to have something totally different that is important."

Nor do all NFL fathers try to be home as much as they can during the season. A minority of coaches and players remain at work even longer than necessary because they don't really want to be home. Raising kids is itself a tough, sometimes frustrating job, and they'd rather not deal with it. Others overwork because they feel the traditionally male "pressure to provide," and in the notoriously unstable NFL they feel they are one missed play or one loss away from being cut or fired. If they don't go home but stay at the facility to be productive and watch film, they think they will be one up on their opponents.

One coach's wife dissected this parenting dynamic among some coaches, speaking quite emotionally not so much to her own experience as to that of numerous other wives she has known:

If coaches don't go home, they don't have to get into the personal interaction part of raising kids. As long as the kids are making good grades and are catching all the touchdowns and making all the baskets, those are *my* kids. But when it comes time that Johnny is not doing his homework or Johnny is being a mouthy kid at home and is being disrespectful, and the coach's wife says, "I need you to sit down and talk to him; I need you to set up some accountability at home and to support me on this," the coach says, "Well, you know, I've got a meeting."

It is a way to—legitimately, in the men's minds—get out of participating in the difficult parts of life, where Dad is not the good guy or hero.

That is why I get so upset with these guys. If they put themselves into their families more to help solve the problems with the children, if they used their ability to focus and analyze and come up with a plan—or the new word they love so much, scheme—then our children would have a relationship with their dads. When the players got on TV, they would say, "Hi, Dad" and not "Hi, Mom." The reason they say "Hi, Mom" is because she has been there.

On the other hand, some wives, like Pat Kennan and Lori Warhop, feel that seeing the dedication of fathers to their jobs can teach children valuable life lessons. Though Lori jokes that her coach husband only sees her and their kids in their pajamas, she says, "The children see their father work very hard. Even though they're really young, we still talk to them about being on time. 'Daddy can't stay and play another game with you because he has to be at work at 10 because he has a meeting.' Those things show good character."

Families in Transition

Family life during the NFL season is hard. But life during the off-season can be even more unsettling. At the very least, the transition from preoccupied, beat-up player and absentee coach to active, dutiful husband and father is rarely smooth.

During the season, NFL women have done nearly everything on the home front. They have planned and orchestrated every domestic and social activity, large and small—and most often without any feedback or assistance from their partners. Once a coach or player has decompressed emotionally and recovered physically from the grueling season, he often responds by overcompensating for his absence. Some feel guilty for all the time spent away from home, and they shower their children with extravagant toys and gifts to make up for it. Others return to the fold and become overinvolved and domineering. Fighting and miscommunication between NFL couples, especially related to child rearing, are common at the beginning of the off-season.

One coach's wife says, "For wives it's like, 'This is my turf! Who are you? You have not been here for how many months, and you want to tell somebody WHAT?' The guys came back, and they really didn't know how to act. They didn't know the family's customs. They didn't know the language. They weren't familiar with the slang. They were total foreigners. My husband would come back into the home and think he had an established position, but he really didn't, because he was never really there to establish it all those other months."

A player's wife said that every off-season she felt the same as a wife in a retired couple. Now, she says, the husband's "home all the time, and he comes in and tells her how to do things, which she has been doing for thirty years. I get a little bit touchy about certain things. This is how I did it while you were playing football, so don't come and tell me I need to load the dishwasher this way, 'cause it was loaded fine during the fall. The off-season is an adjustment."

Lori Warhop says she and her husband George plan "revolving dates" with their daughter and son to help smooth the off-season transition and to create valuable one-on-one time with Dad. She says, "One Saturday George and Olivia will spend the day together, and the following Saturday, George and Jacob will go somewhere to be together. When he is with Olivia, I'm with Jacob, and when he is with Jacob, I'm with Olivia. We have time together as a family, but I also think it's important that their father spends individual time with them."

Clearly, as another coach's wife explained, it's not just husband and wife who have to adjust to parenting together again. The kids have their own agendas and adjustments to make. She says:

When the kids were young, they loved the off-season. Dad only did fun stuff with them. But when they became teenagers, they were like, "Why do we have to talk to Dad?" They had their little social schedules and their church schedules, so we had our routine, and Dad was never a part of that. The only thing

Dad was a part of is when we went to the game and we saw Dad. And we saw him at dinner after the game and maybe sometimes on Saturdays a little bit for a home game.

But when the season was over, and he was actually home for dinner during the week, they already had their schedules. They were popping in and out, and Dad was like, "So when is somebody going to come talk to me?" To him, I'd say, "This is how we do things. Plug yourself in where you think you can fit." And to the kids, I would say, "Go in there and tell your dad what you are doing." They would say, "What? Oh gosh. Why?" They didn't see any reason for it. But my role was to make sure that we all interacted with each other and included Dad, because otherwise kids will be kids. They do what they do because Dad did what he did. I was the coordinator. I coordinated.

The transition from the off-season back to the regular season can be just as difficult. In fact, several coaches' wives said that special treatment from Dad in the off-season upsets the children even more dramatically when the season starts. After finally getting comfortable and feeling secure in their father's presence, these kids are absolutely crushed when he is ripped away yet again.

Some kids react by clinging to their mothers, who are their only constant, and rejecting their fathers when they are home. Other children express their feelings of abandonment by acting out negatively. One player's wife said she noticed her five-year-old daughter becoming rebellious after her husband went away to training camp. She says, "At first, I thought, no way is she really reacting to her dad being gone, but she wasn't listening to me and she was talking back. Then when my husband came home after training camp . . . back to normal. My husband and I asked a few other wives, and they said the same, exact thing."

One coach's wife has developed a strategy for smoothing over this transition back to the season: "When Dad goes to training camp, I take the kids to 'fun camp' with our relatives back East. They have a great time with the relatives; then when the kids come back home, they are excited to play with their friends. Then school starts, and they are excited for that. I schedule things so they don't have time to miss their dad. You have got to keep them busy."

Defensive Line or Delivery Room?

Not just raising but even *having* children presents its own difficulties for NFL families. One of the biggest worries for NFL mothers-to-be—but for players' wives in particular—is whether a partner will be present for a baby's birth. Teams strongly discourage and also fine players for missing games, but coaches also feel pressure not to miss a game, particularly since there is no one who can replace them on the sidelines. If babies are not carefully timed for the off-season, there is a chance NFL women will deliver alone.

It is not uncommon to read a newspaper article sometime during the football season discussing this situation. Shockingly, the tone of the articles is often critical of the pregnant woman: If Mrs. Tight End goes into labor on game day, should her husband stay in the game or go to the hospital? If he left the game, wouldn't he be deserting his team? Doesn't he have a sense of responsibility to his teammates? Couldn't she have planned it better not to interfere with a game?

Didn't anyone ever tell these reporters it takes two to make a baby?

In fact, if a player doesn't suit up, his fears that a replacement player could show up and do a better job, thereby taking over his position, are valid. And his team might indeed have a better chance of winning with him in action. Still, some players say, "Forget it." They refuse to step on the field if it is likely that their wives will give birth on game day. These players accept fans' wrath and their team's fine to take their place by their wives' side.

If a baby is due during the season, it's more common for athletes to suit up and simply gamble that the game will end before the delivery begins and that they will make it to the hospital in time. Some, however, willingly place the game before the wonder of their child's birth. Early on, they inform the pregnant woman they cannot, or will not, miss a game. Basically, she is on her own.

One player's wife said her husband told her that when the time came, his priority would be to play football. She says, "That really is hard on a family because you're sacrificing watching your child come into the world for a job that is incredible. But it's so hard because you almost wonder, Are you going to regret this twenty years from now? Was it really worth missing the birth of my child?"

Another player's wife says, "I was already in labor, and I was in the hospital watching him on television. He was in the huddle, and he was like, 'Okay guys, my wife is having a baby. We've got to hurry up and get this game over with so I can go.' "

During the season, it is relatively common for NFL women to induce labor on a prearranged day once their due date has arrived or passed to ensure their husbands will be present. Some pregnant women have even scheduled C-sections.

Kim Ruddy says, "Our son was due smack dab in the middle of camp. Thank God in a way, and not thank God in another way, that he came early. But our son did make it home before camp started. My daughter was born the night before we played Buffalo right smack dab in the season. Tim had to miss his meeting to be there. It was quite interesting. I said [to the baby], 'You had better hurry, or he is going to be gone.' "

Kim says that if she'd had to, she would have induced labor, so long as it was safe. "Your baby is only born once, and I would much rather that my husband be there for that moment in life, which can never be relived, than to miss it because I wouldn't let my doctor take control. Would I have a C-Section for it? No."

Similarly, another player's wife says, "I didn't induce with my daughter, but I've heard of women who do. I wouldn't want to do that because I wouldn't want to mess with nature in that way. I heard of women doing that because they wanted their husbands to be present at the birth, and I can totally understand that. I wouldn't want my husband to miss that either."

Still, no woman wants her child's birth to compete with a football game, and most NFL couples try to plan their kids' birthdays — not to mention weddings and any other major life events — within the off-season window of February through mid-July. As any couple who has tried to have a baby knows, however, nothing is guaranteed.

The timing of our little Baby Bye Week (the nickname we gave to our baby because she was conceived during the Raiders' Bye Week) could not have been more perfect. Our daughter arrived in the off-season two days before John's summer vacation, and he was able to spend five joyous weeks bonding with the chubby-cheeked light of his life. Besides cooking for an exhausted first-time mom, the daddy dearest changed hundreds of diapers, ran multiple baths, and swaddled over and over until he had the perfect little burrito baby. It was a valuable time of togetherness and learning for us all (although the coach never did stop calling her pacifier a "mouthpiece").

We were very lucky. Because our baby was born in the off-season, John never had to agonize about whether I would go into labor minutes after the team departed for an East Coast game, and I didn't have to worry about fumbling for a cell phone to tell him the good news in the minutes after our daughter arrived.

But Mother, I Love Him!

In today's highly mobile society, many families deal with moving at some point, but few do it as frequently and regularly as NFL families. The nearest comparison is probably military life, and army brats and NFL kids do tend to grow up with similar issues and strengths. They tend to mature more quickly, learn to make friends readily, and consider the world their home.

For the more established players' families, moving is usually a matter of going between a rented in-season home and a more "permanent" off-season address. This biannual change of scenery can be rough on young children. Disruptions in sleeping patterns and potty training regression are among the difficulties wives have noted. One veteran player's wife maintained two households until it became too much of a "hassle."

She says, "It's like all I did was pack and unpack. When we rented, it was like living in a hotel or like camping. We had rented furniture, and we had four dishes. It was yucky. It was okay for me, but for the girls, it was like, 'Where are our toys? Where is our room? Where is all our stuff?' "

During the off-season, some players are away for long stretches attending team workouts. If these off-season separations become hard on the kids, the solution is to live near the team year round. Eventually many players and their families choose to make the in-season home their "permanent" address.

In the case of less stable players and the coaches throughout the league NFL moves are often precipitated by a firing. When this occurs, parents need to be very careful how they present the situation to their children. Kids do not grasp the concept of the NFL as a business; instead, they see firings as a personal attack against their fathers. NFL couples are normally angry when the husband is cut, and in private if not in public they may bad-mouth the team or coach that released him. But where adults can eventually put aside their hurt and anger and move on, kids take it more personally. It can be damaging for them to think their dad was fired because the team no longer likes him.

One coach's wife says, "They need to know that Dad is okay. They are worried about how their dad is going to feel, and that might be the reason they get upset."

Gay Nell Shaw talked about coaching her kids in how to respond to their peers. She says, "It was my job to put a reality spin on it so that my kids knew what was real. Sometimes I would ask them if anything was said to them, so I could help them with a response. There were also times when I would tell them not to respond at all. I always told them, 'You do not have to defend your father.' I wouldn't let them be put in that place because it's just not fair to them. I would just say, 'Oh, man, it's no big deal. Dad is going to get another job.' Or if I knew that he already had another job: 'Oh, we get to move!' I put it in a positive way."

When kids are little, it is easier to make moving seem like an adventure. It is easier to simply say, "Oh, we get to move!" without explaining why. Children have fewer friends, and they make new ones more readily.

As kids get older, moving is proportionally more difficult. They are more invested in their lives—they play on sports teams and participate in school activities; they have established friends and sometimes their first serious romances. Starting over in a new town can come to seem like the end of the world. With typical teenage angst, some kids threaten to run away from home rather than uproot again. I've heard of some parents who—if their child was absolutely dead set against moving—allowed the child to live with a friend's family until graduation, but no NFL women to whom I spoke said they would do that.

One NFL mother says, "One move was especially hard. It was the end of my daughter's junior year of high school. She was dating this kid that I didn't like, so I was happier than hell to be moving. But she was a little defiant, and she would not go with me to pick out the new house."

Gay Nell Shaw feels that the most difficult part of being in the NFL for her kids was "moving every three years." Still, she feels very strongly that she would never let her home be split:

> Keeping my family together was everything to me. I felt the family was more important than the friendships. I would not entrust my child to learn or to be influenced by someone else's mores, their values. I wouldn't do it. I didn't give my kids the choice. What I did to make it as palatable as possible was to make the kids part of the process: they looked for the new house. They would go with me on a visit where the new place was. We would get in the car, and I'd say, "Let's go get lost. Let's go find our way around." Whether they enjoyed it or not, they were part of the process.

Getting a consistent education is also tough, both for a player's kid, who splits schools between the in- and off-season, and for a coach's kid, who must adapt to a new school every couple of years. Schools, teachers, and curricula can vary a great deal, and NFL kids are often either struggling to catch up or are too advanced for their class and are bored.

Many of the women to whom I spoke indicated that personality largely determines how a child is affected by his or her family's relocation. If a shy child doesn't adapt well to change, moving might be emotionally detrimental. On the other hand, being forced to make friends in different social settings could help this same child become more outgoing. The majority of NFL coaches' kids I have known are remarkably confident and well spoken, and they are not easily intimidated by social situations. They can look anyone in the eye and carry on a conversation, whether it's with another child or an adult, the coach's secretary or the team's owner.

Kathy Waufle believes that because of her family's repeated moves, both her daughters matured faster than their peers, making them self-reliant and "better prepared for their future"—although

Kathy admits that her elder daughter had a more difficult time than her younger.

Kathy says, "Moving has taught them to be fighters and how to establish themselves because they had to go in there and be strong and meet new friends. Every time you meet new people, the more personalities you learn to deal with."

Another positive of moving is that it exposes kids to different cultures and regions of the country, thereby making them more socially conscious and aware. Coach's wife Gay Nell Shaw has definitely turned moving and dealing with new and unfamiliar environments into a positive for her children:

We are black. Every time we moved, it was into a white neighborhood. We would find the best school and the best house we could afford, and it was always in a white neighborhood. I would make sure that I would find a big, good black church that had a youth group that my kids could plug into, so that they would feel comfortable. That would help them with their sociability. Then we would get active and do whatever there was to do. I always had them play parks-and-recreation sports. I made sure that they got involved right away, because once you become part of a team or a club you have an immediate connection with people, and you will make at least one friend. Because if you don't make kids do it, they are going to sit and whine and complain. I am not going to hear it. This is our life. This is the way we have to live it.

As a result of all their moves, Gay says the following of her kids:

They are accepting of people for who they are instead of what they look like. They are probably less likely to be prejudiced because they have seen both sides. For instance, we lived in Arizona, and the schools would bus in American Indian kids from the reservations. When my daughter was in fourth grade, she came home and told me a joke about Indians. She was laughing. I listened, and then I asked her why she thought it was funny. She said she really didn't know. So I changed the joke up and made it a joke about black people. And it wasn't funny anymore.

My kids have lived around. They are one race, and I made sure they didn't lose that. They always knew where they came from. But they always saw the people they were dealing with for who they were and where they came from. This came from a saying my mother gave me: "If you want to understand a person, look from whence they came." It's personalities that blend. My kids have always had eclectic friends.

Quick! Burn the Sports Pages

Just as NFL wives enter the public eye because of their husbands' jobs, so do NFL kids, who must learn to deal with all the reflected attention that entails, both good and bad.

Entering a new school as a football kid makes some children instant celebrities, and being seen as "special" can make it easier for them to make friends and be accepted. Their classmates may just think they're cool, or they may secretly hope to attend a pro game or get a player's autograph.

Most NFL moms to whom I spoke said they didn't try to warn their children about people who might try to take advantage of them only to get closer to their fathers or to the NFL. They said that this sense of caution was something kids learned themselves. The majority of players' kids are too young to be suspicious about people's true intentions. Older kids, whether those of coaches or players, learn to be wary through experience.

One coach's wife described her astonishment when her son's teacher asked him for game tickets. She says, "My son had just started this school a couple weeks prior. What was he supposed to say? It was his teacher! How does a twelve-year-old say no to his teacher? I was pissed at the teacher for putting my son on the spot. It's sad because you want your kids to be open and free. Now my son keeps very quiet about what his dad does for a living. I don't blame him."

A celebrity kid can also become a target for envy and jealousy. Especially after their dads have had a losing game or season, NFL kids often must suffer the cruel remarks and taunts of other kids.

This happens in every school and to every kid at some point, and there is not much parents can do.

Of interactions on the schoolyard, a coach's wife says, "I have seen too many kids suffer. The players' kids are very small, and they are out of it before they have really grown up in it. My children have had a lot of mean kids saying things to them at school, like, 'Your dad stinks. He should be fired. He is the worst defensive coordinator ever.' I mean just a lot of nasty comments. It is because of this that our kids do not go to the games; they don't need to hear it there as well."

Indeed, it's not just at school that kids have to deal with fallout from their fathers' jobs. Whether attending a game or watching it on TV, they witness how fans feel about their fathers. Most NFL mothers said they did everything possible to avoid exposing their children to fan abuse and public criticism of their fathers. After a loss, some mothers do not let their kids read potentially degrading newspaper articles, listen to sports talk radio, or watch the highlights on the sports channels.

According to one coach's wife, "I don't want them hearing negative things about their dad or other coaches they know. Even though it is not their dad, it is their dad's friend or their mom's friend."

Gay Nell Shaw has a different perspective:

I never told them to not watch or read anything. What I told them was that this was not personal. These people do not know your father. They do not know Willie Shaw. They have never come over to our house and sat down and had coffee with us. And if you do hear them, I don't want you to ever say anything to them.

When we were at the games, I used to tell my kids to stay incognito. Don't let anybody know that you are his child. Let them say what they want to say. They paid their $59. Football is the everyday man's way of getting out his aggression. He can go to war every Sunday. When they say those horrible things and when they are cussing and being degrading, it isn't really your dad [they are targeting]. It isn't really who they are either. When they leave there, they are probably really nice people.

But they get to do this free-wheeling with no consequence. They just want their team to win.

Of course, children can sense when their parents are tense, stressed, or upset. No matter how well parents shield their kids from the comments of others, there is no hiding at home. When a father greets his kids after a losing game, try as he might, he is not as happy as after a win.

One NFL wife says, "My kids know that when their dad comes off the field and he hasn't won, he just needs a great, big hug. He even tells them, I needed a hug when I was standing down on the field."

Players' injuries affect kids, too. It is nearly impossible for fathers to hide their physical pain when, after the game, their hands are swollen and bandaged and ice packs are wrapped around every joint. Kids quickly learn that Dad can't wrestle or play with them because he hurts.

One player's wife says it's important to be honest about injuries: "When he comes home, they need to know why he is hurt, and that is the reason why he doesn't want to play with them."

Kim Ruddy says that injuries to their father "affect my kids a lot emotionally. They don't understand it."

NFL moms wrestle with how much or how little to explain to their kids. In part, the age of the child is a factor, but Kathy Waufle believes overprotecting kids can be harmful. She says, "There are certain things that you don't want kids to know and hear, but overall, you should let them know it is a very high-pressure, tense job. It's really weird how children perceive things, and you don't want to put the wrong impression in their heads. Honesty, to a certain degree, is best."

Boys Play Football and Girls Are Cheerleaders

With the public's and a family's constant focus on the father and his job, it is easy for some NFL kids to identify so fully with their dads that they have a hard time developing personalities of their own. Some kids, particularly boys, go full throttle into their dads' careers. These pint-sized football junkies are often compulsive overachievers. Going far beyond the win/loss record, these kids can recite individual and team statistics better than the players or coaches. In the stands, these diminutive fanatics shriek their lungs out when a referee makes a bad call against their dad or the team. Their little faces light up in joy when their dad's team wins, but after a loss, these same youngsters are left in tears, dragging their tiny sneakers through the stadium exit doors.

One coach's wife says, "When we lost the Super Bowl, it was real hard for my eight-year-old. When his dad came out of the locker room, I told him right away that his son was crying because of the loss. At that point, his father knew it wasn't about him; it was about his kid. I try to catch their dad ahead of time on things like that."

Of her children's reaction to a loss, another coach's wife says, "Sometimes, I think they were more embarrassed. They thought that the next day at school, they would not be the heroes of the day. If we won, they could really strut their stuff in school. If they lost, they kind of had to sneak into school."

Conversely, with all the attention lavished upon their fathers—people asking for their autographs, putting them on a pedestal and talking about how "special" they are—some kids become exceedingly shy. They feel smaller or less important than their dads. These sensitive youngsters often retreat into their own self-contained cocoon.

For some reason, many people assume and expect NFL kids will excel at football (and other sports) too—no matter the child's athletic ability or preference for other things. Boys are exposed to the strategy of the game, and they are also encouraged to develop their own physical talent. If these kids, particularly players' sons, are not good athletes, failing to measure up to their fathers on the playing field can strike their self-esteem hard.

A player's wife described the classic situation: "I have two boys, and people say to them, 'I bet you can't wait to grow up and be just like dad.' One of the boys has no athletic ability, and I think he'll be a bookworm, but people think he should be just like dad. The other one is very much like dad. Still, I won't encourage football."

Jackie Rice says that people put the same athletic expectations on her son, "especially since he has the same name as his dad." She adds:

During the summertime, when the kids go to particular sports camps, it is so funny watching other kids' reactions. When they have to separate into different groups and [the coaches] call them by name, saying "Jerry Rice Jr.," all the kids just turn around and look. He is like, "Oh, my."

But he deals with the pressure very well because he is a great athlete. He does have a God-given ability and an inherited ability, but he doesn't have to be this super-duper football player like his dad. That is not something that we expect of him. We tell the kids that all the time: they can do whatever they choose to do as long as it is something that will grant them success. Being successful at something and loving what you do—to me, that is the most important thing, loving what you do. In this day and age, in the time that we live, there are so many opportunities for kids, especially for African American kids. Back then, when my husband was growing up, the only way you could probably see your way out of anything was sports, but nowadays that is different.

Girls are fortunate, in a way. They don't have as much pressure to measure up to dear old dad. But this is changing. Females are increasingly participants in the NFL's Punt, Pass and Kick contests, which are national skills competitions for boys and girls ages 8–15. The NFL also offers NFL Flag, which is the league's official nationwide youth football league for boys and girls ages 6–14. And in a wide range of sports beyond football—basketball, soccer, softball, track and field, and more—women are respected as athletes almost as much as men.

Jackie Rice says that her oldest daughter receives the same pressure from others to excel in sports as her son does: "Our oldest daughter is an athlete. She played volleyball, ran track, played basketball, but the past several years she decided that singing was what she wanted to do. That is where her true love is. Of course you have those people who say, 'That is Jerry Rice's daughter. She has got to be this, she has got to play,' or whatever. We have just always let the kids make their choice."

Nevertheless, with no role models on the professional football field (despite a stray woman photographer on the sidelines once in a while), players' and coaches' daughters have no one to emulate—apart from team cheerleaders. And emulate them they do; indeed, six-year-old girls can be seen in the stands closely imitating the oversexed shake and shimmy of pom-poms.

Another way in which boys and girls are treated differently is that boys are sometimes allowed at their fathers' sides, while girls are always on the sidelines. In the stands, all children are lucky to have opportunities to socialize with big-name players and occasionally meet famous people (such as movie and music stars who attend games), but only boys are allowed in the locker room after a game. This is a favorite pastime of many players' and coaches' sons, who then get to walk out of the stadium with their dads.

One player's wife says, "They get to see a whole other side of sports that a lot of people in the world don't. They get to see behind the scenes that so many young kids would love to see. I think that is cool. I think it's more exciting for an NFL boy than it is for an NFL wife."

Another wife described a little of the post-game locker room atmosphere: "The guys go around and hit [my son] on the head when they walk by. They know he is a kid. I am sure he is going to hear language that he shouldn't hear, but hopefully he knows enough to not repeat that language later. He gets autographs, and he talks to the players, but he knows whom he can approach and whom he cannot."

However, not every parent thinks the locker room is an appropriate place for children, as is the case for one coach's wife: "I never let them go, and their father never encouraged it. It is an adult male place. That is the bottom line. They don't need to go in there. Those are men from God knows where and God knows what backgrounds. I don't know if they are family men. All I know is they were just out there cussing and grunting and trying to kill each other. I don't want my boys around that."

The sons of coaches can also be with their fathers at work during training camp. When boys are old enough, usually around ten (or when their fathers feel they can handle themselves if left alone), and as long as the head coach approves, sons can come and watch training camp. Many take on gopher-type duties like collecting balls for the kickers and punters and helping the equipment managers.

Young kids might stay only three or four days, but older boys might stay for the entire camp. Girls are not granted any similar privilege.

Well-Adjusted, Independent, Yet Humble

Raising level-headed, mature NFL kids is not an easy task. Few children outside of professional sports witness their dads being begged for autographs by adoring fans. There are fewer yet who can claim that in a nation that worships its sports stars, their dads are among them. Some NFL moms with whom I spoke worried openly that all the attention, and in some cases their wealthy lifestyles, would create spoiled, self-involved children.

Moms who had already raised NFL kids said it was very important that their children's lives did not revolve around their dads' jobs. Self-identity issues arise when children become overly invested in and have a difficult time separating from their fathers' careers.

When Kathy Nolan, the wife of a coach and mother of four, wants to watch her husband's team play on television, she goes into a separate room from her children.

She says, "If they want to watch a movie or Disney, I am not going to make them watch the football game. I don't want to force them to be interested in something they don't care about. Frankly, if it was a good game, they are going to be all high. But if it was a bad game, they would be sitting there thinking, 'Uh-oh, Daddy is going to be sad.' In their world, they are just as happy, so why involve them?"

Many three-year-olds—whether they have NFL dads or not—exclaim, "I want to be a football player when I grow up." This is normal. But as children get older, NFL moms agree that they must work extra hard to widen their scope beyond the football field. Kids need to find *their* passion, and it can be difficult when their fathers cast a large shadow.

This has certainly been the case for Kim Singletary's two oldest kids. She says, "Up until Kristin was seventeen and Matt was fourteen, they struggled with being underachievers. We didn't know why. We thought, they have done everything. They have been everywhere. They have met everyone. What nine-year-old has been to Hawaii nine times, you know? We just didn't know if they couldn't find their own thing to get motivated about or if it was just their personality. Mike and I were always curious. They were around through all the Bears' hoopla and everything, and they were such underachievers. When we moved to Baltimore in 2002, we decided to put them both back a grade."

Kim says everything has changed in their new hometown. She says their neighborhood isn't crazy about sports, and in Baltimore, "Ray Lewis is God. Mike is really nothing here."

As a result, Kim says:

Matt became Matt. He thrived. All A's. Before we moved, every teacher from kindergarten through ninth grade said, "I tell you what, this is a brilliant kid." I was so sick of hearing that when he had D's and F's. I didn't even know if I believed it anymore. He comes here and gets all A's. The pressure is off.

And Kristin just kind of got to be Kristin, too. She was riding being "Mike Singletary's daughter." Where Matt was trying to find Matt, Kristin was a little too comfortable in that role. The move itself was wonderful for our family. Both of them have found themselves, found their niche, taken responsibility for their education. It is not about Mike, because it is about Ray here, which works wonderfully for them. It was really good.

Clearly NFL kids often live vastly different lives than their parents did growing up. Some NFL parents came from impoverished or lower-middle-class homes. Even if a player does not count himself among the multimillion dollar superstar athletes, he and his family may be considerably wealthier than they were before the NFL. No matter what their individual income, all families are exposed to a sophisticated lifestyle and high-profile world that may be miles away from the small towns they came from. Despite their best efforts to keep their kids humble, some NFL mothers expressed concern about the effects of wealth and privilege on their kids.

One player's wife says, "You try to keep a balance so they're not spoiled and think they're entitled to all these things. When I grew up and we asked for things, my parents said, 'We can't afford that.' But I can't say that to them because you want to be truthful with them. We try really hard to keep them grounded and not think that they're special because of the NFL. They're special because they're great kids but not special because of who their dad is."

Gay Nell Shaw admits that it can be very difficult at times, since children are naturally competitive with each other:

We lived in better neighborhoods than most of the kids they knew. We drove a better car. We always had nice clothes and nice things. They were used to having better than the average. When we would go visit families, many times I would have to prepare them for what we were going into and talk to them about being blessed and being fortunate because of what Dad did. These people didn't have the opportunity to make that kind of money, so you don't flaunt it. You don't make people feel bad or look down on people.

I will say, look, your father is the one who struggled. He went to school and he worked and he got his education. I will tell them his background; I will say, this is how we got to the point that we could afford this. He bought this. This does not belong to you. It is not yours. When my kids were growing up, I did not allow them to have everything that we could afford. They did not have their own phone in their room; they did not have their own TV. We could afford those things, but they didn't earn them. I tried to teach my kids to stay real.

There were occasions where they got on their high horse. "We got this and you don't," and I would slap them right down as soon as I saw it because I know from whence we came. They did have a lot, but nothing turned me off more than a snob. But sometimes my kids would get snobby. "Your stuff ain't as good as my stuff." It is something that you have to stay alert to. And as a mother and a wife, you have to watch how you do it, too.

In this day and age, NFL women are also aware that high-profile or perceived-to-be-rich people are more open to kidnapping or abduction. Such fears are not widespread, but they do exist. One well-known player's wife said she was extremely conscious about her kids' not bragging about *anything*. "People are strange. You never know what they are thinking," she explains warily.

Another player's wife says, "Yes, we have avoided publicity in order to protect our privacy. Absolutely, with our kids especially. It's very hard to be in the public eye when you have children. There are a lot of weird people in the world, and you just have to protect your kids. There have been opportunities for the kids to do things, but I've kind of held them back from doing them."

Despite their material possessions and the public attention given to the NFL, NFL kids still seem to take their behavioral cues from their parents. Children with the best sense of balance about NFL life have parents who achieved their own sense of balance first. For instance, when Kathy Nolan talks to her kids about their father's work, she praises the job he does without glorifying football. This is how Kathy and her husband help their four kids stay grounded.

She explains, "We say it's Daddy's job, and we try to keep it separate, so that everything does not revolve around his job. It revolves around 'this is a family, and this is how he supports us.' Not as a knock on it, but not to glorify it and make it about how other people think it is. People say, 'Oh my gosh, that's so neat.' And it is neat. But it's not everything. So we try to keep it normal. We have taught the kids that there is absolutely nobody better than them, but there is nobody worse than them, either. That is important. They know no matter what people's jobs are, they are respected and honored for what they do."

Kim Singletary exemplifies this perspective quite humbly and elegantly. She says: "I have put the responsibility on our kids to uphold the reputation that Mike has built—not in a 'What would people think' way, but in a 'What we represent' way. Our kids have been very normal kids—they have failed—and I think that is actually encouraging to people. We did not have perfect kids, and we never tried to create an air of perfection. We tried to create an air of responsibility. We tell them, 'You have been very blessed, and in turn, you be a blessing.'"

Big Time Money? Not for Everyone **8**

An NFL woman can sense it coming. First, it's the "No, really?" when another woman finds out she is married to an NFL player or coach, and it is followed by the quick head-to-toe once-over. Then it's the skeptical look of surprise after the observer sees her pretty, yet many times average-sized, diamond ring. It's almost as if people think an NFL woman's knuckles should be dragging the ground with the weight of the gem.

After describing this common experience to me, one NFL woman said, "I can't necessarily blame them, you know. I thought the same thing."

There are a few persistent misperceptions about life in the NFL, and one of them is that everyone employed by the sport is ultra-rich. Everyone isn't, and this news is frequently greeted with surprise and skepticism—and even at times with what seems like disappointment. For some, the NFL is their ultimate fantasy of glamour, wealth, and the good life, and they don't really want to hear that it can sometimes be quite the opposite.

The media do a tremendous job of hyping the highest NFL player salaries. In fact, according to the NFLPA, there are basically two groups of players in the league: starters and nonstarters; the "middle class" just doesn't exist. According to M. J. Duberstein of the NFLPA research department, "If you look at averages by year in the league, you see a huge jump once players are able to be free agents — now, after four accrued seasons. This means that half of the players have very little market power and half do."

The majority of players are not making millions every year, and NFL coaches — except for a handful of veteran head coaches — make significantly less than players. When you consider that the average NFL player's career lasts just over three years, it becomes clear why only a handful of players leave the NFL "set for life." Most ex-players, particularly if they haven't managed their money well, are looking for a new job not long after hanging up their cleats.

None of this is to deny that, compared to those in other professions, NFL players and coaches make a good living, one that's often better — at times far better — than most. But there are wide disparities of income in the league, and the often short, unreliable nature of employment means that there are no guarantees. If it comes, the "good life" usually lasts only a couple of years. Some choose to live large while they can, and some save for the fast-approaching day when the NFL decides a player's services are no longer needed.

Players: Making Millions or the Minimum?

NFL players get paid well for what they do, but most of them don't take home as much as people think. Here is a look at some typical salaries and contracts.

In 2003, the minimum salary (what's called the "league minimum") for an NFL player was $225,000 in his first year. After the first year, the league minimum rises based on the number of years in service. After one year, it's $300,000; after two years, $375,000; after three years, $450,000; after four years (and through the seventh year), $525,000; after seven years (and through the tenth year), $650,000. These numbers, which typically rise by a few thousand dollars every year, are set by contract between the NFL and the NFLPA.

Except for first-round draft picks, nearly every new NFL rookie player makes the league minimum. However, signing bonuses vary widely and depend largely on the round in which a player is selected. First-round picks will make around $280,000 per year in salary, with a signing bonus ranging from $20 million at the top of the round to about $5 million at the bottom. Many second-round picks will receive the minimum $225,000 salary with a $1 to $3 million signing bonus, and third-round picks will also receive the minimum salary with a $350,000 to $700,000 signing bonus.

Rookie contracts have typically been for three years, but recently they have been getting longer—up to five or six years—in part so teams can prorate large signing bonuses over a longer time, and in part so teams can keep player salaries lower for longer. With the average playing career lasting just over three years, chances are good that the initial contract will be the first and last contract a player will sign.

The NFLPA does not normally keep track of how many players are making the league minimum in any given year, but it provided the following figures for the year 2000. That season, out of a total of 1,818 players, 352 made the league minimum—that is, almost 20 percent across the NFL. There were 140 first-year players at the minimum, 82 second-year players, 40 third-year players, and 43 players with over six years of league tenure.

Finally, rounding out each team are the eight players on the practice squad, each of whom earns $73,950 a year.

Unless players already have four seasons under their jerseys (and thereby become "vested"), their contracts are not guaranteed. In addition, in order for the contract of a vested player to be guaranteed, he must be on the roster for the first game of the season. Teams sometimes take advantage of this loophole and minimize the number of guaranteed contracts they have to sign by cutting certain veterans before the season starts and then re-signing them after the first game. Nonvested players can be cut at any time, and the NFL does not have to pay them another dime.

Injuries can also devastate a player's career. For a rookie struggling to establish himself, his contract is only as good as his last game. At any moment, on any play, he could break an arm, be put on injured reserve, and then, when he is deemed healthy, be released—even if he is in the first year of a multiyear contract. Once a player is released, his entire contract is null and void. Again, unless he is vested—in which case his health insurance carries over for one year—once a player is cut, he receives no income and no benefits. In the case of guys who have "guaranteed" contracts—usually first-round draft picks and high-profile players—only a percentage of the contract is actually guaranteed, rarely the full amount.

In today's salary-capped NFL, many of the veteran players' long-term contracts are also "backloaded." That means that the bulk of the salary is paid out near the end of the contract, not at the beginning. For example, say a player signs a five-year, $27 million deal. This level of salary is typical of a high percentage of veteran free agents. The player may receive $1 million as a signing bonus and a first-year salary of $500,000; that's a total of $1.5 million for the first year. The second year he is scheduled to get $3 million; the third year, $5 million; the fourth year, $7 million; and the fifth year, $10.5 million. This is backload. The team could cut the guy after the first year and be out only $1.5 million. This example is typical of what "guaranteed money" means in the NFL—it is the up-front cash found in the signing bonus.

Some contracts come with incentive clauses. This means that in order to make the top amount of a contract—for that top-line player, his full $5 million a year—he must meet certain performance goals, such as catching a certain number of passes, making the Pro Bowl, playing a minimum number of games, and so on. These incentives are often deliberately hard to reach, and they are not always within the player's control. If a coach doesn't run plays for a receiver, how can the receiver make his incentive? The various incentives make it nearly impossible to obtain the entire amount written in a contract.

On top of this, a player has to pay his agent, who typically makes 3 percent of everything the player earns. Then there are taxes, which—depending on marital and homeowner status and the state in which a player resides—can range from 35 to 47 percent for the top-earning players and from 25 to 27 percent for undrafted rookies. Union dues are $10,000 per year, and if a player decides to contribute to this retirement fund, his 401K contributions are $13,000. One often overlooked expense is the cost of game tickets for family and friends. Sometimes $4,000 to $5,000 per year is deducted from players' checks to cover this cost. Other yearly or seasonal expenses could include $3,000 to $5,000 for personal trainers and $2,000 to $3,000 for massage therapy.

All things considered, at the end of the day, a player will very likely bring home less than 50 percent of his gross pay.

However, how much money a player ultimately takes home is usually a concern only for the player himself. All anyone else cares to talk about—and that includes the media, the public, and the players—is the size of the signed contract. Players pay very close attention to the contracts of other players, and the differing salaries within the league create their own problems. They even sometimes impact the plays that are called on the field. Kim Singletary has seen huge changes in the NFL because of money and because of the celebrity that follows big dollars—a situation that she feels has made players in the NFL "too level-oriented, instead of team-oriented." She says it wasn't always this way:

> When we went to the Super Bowl, it was probably the greatest group of characters in the NFL. It was William Perry, Jim McMahon—it was the greatest group of characters, but it was such a team. That is all I knew, but now, I feel that the Play Station, the X-Box, fantasy football—these have made each team have superstars. It completely changes everything when you have a superstar. What does that say to the other ten guys? Put him out there by himself. Let him show how super he is. You start hearing about coaches designing plays around these guys and feeding individual goals.
>
> I just think the differing levels of pay are not good. There might be one out of the eleven players that is content, but it is just human nature to want more. You want what he has. I should be getting what he gets. . . . To me, it just creates division.

Coaches: All Work, Little Pay

Only in recent years have some head coaches been receiving contracts that rival those of the league's star players. According to ESPN.com, Jon Gruden earned over $1 million in endorsements alone in the five months following his Super Bowl XXXVII victory as head coach of the Tampa Bay Buccaneers. For these endorsements, it certainly didn't hurt that Coach Gruden was young and good looking enough to be named one of *People* magazine's "50 Most Beautiful People" in 2001.

But Jon Gruden is one of only a handful of the league's thirty-one head coaches who earns this kind of money. In general, head coaches' annual salaries range from $1 to $5 million. Below the head coach, each team hires approximately sixteen assistant coaches, and they will never see that kind of cash. On average, an entry-level nonposition coach makes $65,000. For a seven-year veteran assistant position coach, salaries average about $245,000 per year.

Without a doubt, coaches' careers last longer than players'. The NFLCA says that on average coaching careers in the NFL last 9.5 years, but my personal experience is that successful NFL coaching careers are often longer—even fifteen to twenty years. Including time spent at the college level, it is not unusual for a coach to enjoy a thirty-year career.

Unlike with players, upon termination, teams generally pay a coach's salary for the length of his contract. However, the coach may not merely sit back and collect his contracted salary. He must search for another job, and if one is offered, he must take the other job to reduce the amount his former team owes him. For example, if a coach was scheduled to make $200,000 and was offered a job for $100,000, he must take that job, and his former team would have to pay him only $100,000. This is commonly referred to as the "offset"—the difference between what he was scheduled to make and what he actually made.

According to the NFLCA, over the past few years teams have creatively—and not so creatively—tried to avoid paying this off-set. Some have deducted playoff bonus money that a coach earned while working for his new team, and some have withheld Super Bowl tickets guaranteed to coaches for each year they coach. Others have simply stopped paying the coach's salary—even for the remainder of the current contract year.

To put coaches' salaries in perspective, consider that in-season they work, on average, eighty to one hundred hours a week, seven days a week. In the off-season they continue to work full-time, but closer to thirty to fifty hours over a five-day week, not including minicamps. When factored on an hourly basis, some coaches don't make any more than typical service sector employees. By comparison, players not only earn much more money, but they are also required to spend far fewer hours, in-season and off-season, at the stadium.

This disparity in salaries between players and coaches is the cause for a whole other set of tensions in the NFL. Of the women with whom I spoke, some coaches' wives considered it unfair, while the majority of players' wives didn't. Players' wives claimed to know little about coaches' salaries, but they also said they didn't think the pay between the two groups should be similar. Never mind a coach's workload, some said—they aren't the ones risking their bodies for "W's." Plus, at best, a player's career will be only one-third the length of a coach's, and, more typically, it will be one-fifth to one-tenth the length.

As one player's wife says, "My husband cannot wear wedding bands because his knuckles have been jammed and his fingers are mangled. He has been told he will probably have to have shoulder replacement surgery. I think the players are making more of a sacrifice physically. Coaches aren't putting their bodies on the line every Sunday, and they don't have the marketing value."

Another player's wife maintained that because of players' shorter careers, coaches "would be able to make more in the long run."

One coach's wife didn't see compensation as a players-versus-coaches issue, but one of overall equity that needed to be addressed by owners. She said, "The coaches do not fall under the whole salary cap issue, so what is the problem? The money is there. The league needs to come up with a collective bargaining agreement for the coaches, something to regulate a certain percentage of salary increase, compensation, and incentives. It is such a huge gap between the coaches and players. I think salaries should be more comparable."

One coach's wife discussed it with her husband, who coaches receivers, and she basically agrees with the players' perspective. She says, "When I talked to my husband about it, he said, 'Nobody comes to see us on Sunday. We're not the ones who are on television. You have to put that into perspective.' So I understand his point. At the same time, when I hear people saying players shouldn't be making that much, I have to disagree. All this money is generated because they are playing this game. Players need to get a cut. Although there is no amount of work that you can do that can justify making $5 million. The reality is that each team controls what coaches make. If you don't want to take it, walk away—most likely you won't."

Because of the hard work of the NFLCA during the past few years, there have been great strides in protecting coaches' rights and better aligning coaches' benefits with those of the players. In the past two years, coaches' salaries have increased rapidly because of the salary information that the NFLCA collects and distributes to its members. But the only way to negotiate league-wide minimum salaries or to get standardized contracts would be for the coaches to form a union. At this time, the NFLCA is not looking to unionize, in part because it doesn't know of an issue of sufficient concern to all of its coaches that it would warrant a strike.

The Blow-Up Mattress Years

Upon "retiring" from his NFL playing career, John Morton accepted a job from owner Al Davis as an intern in the Oakland Raiders' player personnel department. His big-time NFL salary? One hundred and fifty dollars a week. We had some money saved from his playing days but not enough to cover our expenses considering the high cost of living in the San Francisco Bay Area.

For John to accept the low-paying internship, I needed to finish graduate school, follow him to California, and get a job as soon as possible. It was a risky decision. Before joining the World League, John had been working for several months in a stable, nonfootball-related job in Michigan, and John's boss had told him his job would be waiting for him when he returned. The Raiders did not guarantee that John would be hired full-time after the internship. It was considered a tryout of sorts. But with John's rocky and turbulent playing career ending the way it did, his career felt unresolved. If there was a possibility that he could still make his mark in professional sports, he wanted to go for it—but he needed my help.

It's worth remembering—and is another way to put NFL salaries in perspective—that quite a few NFL couples have a similar story to tell about their early days trying to make it in the league. The popular scenario, the one the media highlight, is the rarest: a first-round draft pick immediately signs a multimillion dollar contract out of college, and a few years later, by the time he is twenty-five, his mansion is being profiled on MTV's *Cribs*. This happens, but more commonly a player will spend up to a half dozen years running laps through the league, attending training camps and foreign football leagues.

Salaries and contracts for training camps and in the foreign leagues are minimal. The Canadian Football League salaries for American players can average from $50,000 to $200,000 (quarterbacks get the most money), while the NFL World League contracts are typically around $10,000 for a four-month season.

John and I spent eight months without a phone and slept on a blow-up mattress while he worked his "internship." Among the jobs I took to get us by was driving senior citizens to church. No one would call this glamorous. MTV would not have been interested in our "crib." But a year or two or three like this sticks in the mind of an NFL couple after they've made it in the league. They feel they've paid their dues, and a few years of high salaries and NFL perks doesn't seem quite so extravagant.

Regarding the sometimes envious or even spiteful comments of others, one coach's wife says, "Some people have commented, 'So, what are you driving now?' Or 'Must be nice.' This is what I hear most often. They have no idea that it's taken us ten long years, all of them spent in professional football, before enjoying these extras. Now, when I hear 'Must be nice,' I smile, nod my head, feeling blessed to have come so far, and reply, 'Yes, it is.'"

Spend It or Save It?
Members of the public are not the only ones who think playing in the NFL means instant wealth. Many young players and their families do, too. This expectation can get some young players into financial trouble before they ever receive an NFL paycheck.

One player's wife says, "I've seen where guys come out of college who are not yet drafted, but the agents have told them, 'You're projected to go in this round or that round,' and because of that 'let me go ahead and get you this truck.' The players do not understand that it's a loan. After they get drafted and they get their signing bonus, they have to pay all that back to the agent. But if they don't get drafted, then what? I knew one kid who bought himself and his mom a brand-new car, and then he didn't even make the team. Now he's screwed. He has two car payments and no job. It happens all the time."

Some of the lucky young players who sign their first NFL contracts for hundreds of thousands or perhaps millions of dollars—and then get a big, fat signing bonus to boot—have only one thought: let me spend it as fast as I can. The message these impressionable men receive, fostered mainly by the media, is that to be in the NFL means to live as large as possible. The multimillion dollar homes on *Cribs* are for real. I've visited a few, and they are dizzying. Christmas means twenty-five-foot-tall evergreen trees. Outdoor bamboo gazebos have wall-mounted flat-screen televisions; elevators lead to third-floor beauty salon/barber shops; oversized Jacuzzi tubs are adorned with bath salts the size of golf balls. One NFL woman I know has so many clothes in her closet—the majority with the tags still attached—that she could outfit an entire lower-level section of the Oakland Coliseum.

Even if someone tells these players and their partners that the money will not last forever, they don't listen. Sadly, these *Cribs* moments are often just the first part of a story in money misman-agement. In fact, it's hard to imagine how young men and women could be expected to make smart choices when they seem to have been handed the ultimate fantasy.

Not long after her marriage, a player's wife expressed shock at her mate's spending habits: "He told me that he lent someone $20,000, and at that point I was like, Where are we? What is going on? I thought we were doing fine, but when I finally looked at things, he was paying four mortgages: his mother's; on a house he had bought as an investment; on his first house, from which he'd moved out, but he wasn't being very aggressive about selling it; and on our house. At a certain point, I took over the bills."

Another player's wife admitted, "You get to a point where you have to have a new outfit for every game. I was always shopping. All the time. And I never looked at price tags. It didn't have to be only name-brand, exclusive stuff. I could go to Target. But I never had any regard for what things cost. I really based every purchase on whether I wanted it."

According to one retired player's wife, her husband "bought ten

CDs at the drop of a hat. He had a BMW, an SUV, and my car. He had to have lawn service and a pool cleaner. He would send a limo and airline tickets for friends to come down for a game. He wasn't taught to manage money, and he got caught up in having a particular type of car and house. He had quite a bit of debt. Now that he is out of the game, he wishes he had a second chance to save more."

"I took the money for granted," says another retired player's wife. "I don't know one woman that didn't take money for granted. It would take an incredible amount of discipline not to overspend. Some agents put their guys on budgets, so some of that is done for them, but at some point they need to take on the responsibilities themselves. It would take an incredible amount of discipline not to get caught up."

After her husband Mike had retired, Kim Singletary says, "I was almost embarrassed at my [previous] need for stuff. A fully furnished basement that we used maybe three times per year—but it was so important at the time. The bags and bags and bags of stuff I gave away to cleaning ladies. I was embarrassed at my own lack of regard for it."

And now that Mike is employed again by the NFL? Kim says, "Trust me, on his current coaching salary, I am thinking, 'Okay, do I need it or do I just want it?'"

Whereas some NFL wives and girlfriends are just as eager to spend money as the players, other wives are more sensible, savvy even, especially if their partners have been cut in the past. These women essentially act as their partners' managers. They spend hours on the phone with accountants. They brainstorm with their partners' agents, trying to set up endorsement deals. Most important, these women make sure they will not be caught without reserve money in the bank.

Gina Nedney, whose husband is a punter, says, "Because we have jumped around from team to team in the past and the NFL hasn't always been a stable force in our lives, we save a lot because we don't know when it's going to end. If it were to end tomorrow, we would have enough set aside until we found jobs. We don't live to the point of extravagance, where we couldn't afford our house payment if the NFL ended. When we bought our house, that was our biggest concern. If the NFL stopped tomorrow, could we pay our mortgage with both of us working normal jobs?"

Like Gina, Kathy Nolan, whose husband was a defensive coordinator at the time of our interview, has been with her husband through numerous job changes. Because of this experience, she and her husband want to make sure their family does not get carried away with buying expensive material possessions. For instance, when Kathy's husband was hired by the Redskins as their defensive coordinator, a Washington sports writer took notice . . . of the coach's station wagon. Kathy said the columnist thought it was neat that the high-ranking coach pulled a grocery-getter into the team's parking lot—when the prior coordinator had driven a Porsche.

Kathy says, "Don't get me wrong. I appreciate the really nice things that this life offers, but we are very aware that these things can be gone in an instant. If things change, I don't want us to say, 'Oh, my gosh, we don't know how to live unless we have fancy things.' Mike and I both say, 'Let's live comfortably.' Because if we live above our means, or even within our means at a high level, and those means are gone, what are we going to do?"

Perhaps understandably, some NFL women get defensive about the family income. In most professions, what people earn is considered a private matter, but NFL salaries are published on the Internet, which opens the door to lots of unsolicited advice and opinions.

As one young player's wife aptly puts it: "It hasn't been a problem for us to save money. It's been more of a problem to justify our budgeting to other people. It's such an awkward situation anyway, because they don't feel it rude to ask how much he makes. I say, 'How much do *you* make?' just to show them that the question is inappropriate. You can get on the Web and figure it out. We're just not going to tell them."

When Family and Friends Come Calling

One player's wife and her husband (whom I'll call Haley and Sean) were incredulous when, while Sean was still in college, his parents asked if his first NFL paycheck could go toward paying off their mortgage. Haley says, "They acted like Sean owed them or something."

Many NFL women to whom I spoke had similar stories to tell.

Some stories involved parents who expected their sons to pick up their mortgages or buy them new cars, and others involved friends who had found "great investments" and just needed a little cash. It didn't matter if the player was a practice squad "jake" or an All-Pro vet. Once he had a contract of any kind, family and friends often showed up to request their share. Coaches' wives said they were less likely to get tapped by freeloaders—unless they had recently returned from the Super Bowl—but no one seemed to escape the largely unspoken assumption that when the restaurant tab came, the NFL couple would get it. One coach's wife said her husband's parents and his siblings seemed to have their wallets "glued to their ass" when the bill arrived.

At the time Sean's parents made their request, Sean didn't know if he would be drafted or not. He and Haley were of course hoping that he would be. Based on what his agent had told them, depending on the round, he might receive a contract worth around $600,000 and a signing bonus as high as $100,000.

Sean wasn't drafted, and at that point the odds that he'd make an active roster were piled higher than fat linemen on a fumble. Instead, he became a free agent and signed a $230,000 contract and received a $15,000 signing bonus to attend a team's training camp. The couple's disappointment and surprise continued when, at the end of training camp, Sean did not make the active roster (thereby canceling out the previous quarter-million dollar contract). Instead, he was signed to the practice squad for a yearly salary of $73,950. Sean was now in no position to buy out his parent's mortgage, much less put a sizable down payment on his own house.

Of course, by most standards, $73,950 is a good wage. But it's not a salary that supports an entourage, private limousines, or an entire extended family. The media feed the misperception that all NFL players are rich, and explaining otherwise can be an almost impossible task.

According to numerous women, NFL mothers are especially prone to feeling entitled to their sons' wealth. One player's wife explains: "They don't quite understand that it's not possible for their son to support his wife and children the way he wants to support them and to support his mother on the same level. Some players probably can do it, but they can't all do it that way. [The mothers] don't get how the NFL works as far as the differences in contracts and the differences in lifestyles. I don't think mothers totally understand that their sons can live in a million dollar house and have a couple of cars but that that doesn't necessarily entitle them to the same thing. I would hope that if my children grow up and become successful, I'm not sitting and saying, 'Where's my cut?' "

Another player's wife said she hid her luxury Audi from her jealous mother-in-law for three years, and she still feels the need to censor herself in case her mother-in-law "picks up on it." She says, "You know it's bad when, before you visit your in-laws, you've got to take off your earrings and take off your watch."

In general, it is likely that NFL families are no more or less generous with their money than people in other high-paying professions. However, the family and friends of an experienced computer programmer or lawyer making six figures annually probably don't have the same sense of entitlement toward their incomes. Some may, but probably not with the regularity that NFL women describe. Players and coaches who give into the demands of family when they can't really afford them usually end up in bad situations for everyone. Just ask the former football stars who put twenty of their closest buddies on the payroll, but today those players have to work three menial jobs to pay the bills they accrued.

One player's wife says, "I think a lot of money mismanagement comes as a result of pressure from friends. My husband will go places and meet friends, and everybody has this wonderful idea that just needs some investors. Basically, they want to play with your money. If the investment makes it, then everybody is happy, but if it doesn't, they haven't lost anything; only you have. I think that people play on that. 'Hey, we've been friends for years . . . .' "

Scratching Backs and Quid Pro Quos
Of course, it can work both ways. Businesses big and small like to be affiliated with the NFL, and couples will often use their connection to the NFL to secure bargains, deals, and free services. There are perks to being in the entertainment industry, but sooner or later most NFL families learn that most free offers have a hidden price tag somewhere.

Some businesses see providing NFL players or coaches with free merchandise as good advertising or a way to bring in more customers. Others will say they are just being nice or they want to do a favor. Some people will make fantastic offers simply to get closer to their favorite NFL team or player. It is generally true that if something is for sale—whether it's Christmas trees, new windows, or manicures—NFL families can get it cheaper than others. Only the Rice, Warner, and Gruden families get offered the biggies—like weekend getaways to Pebble Beach golf courses and designer-issued clothing to model—but even the Haleys and Seans of the NFL receive fantastic deals just because of their association with the game.

Some perks are team issued. When the Raiders were in Los Angeles, my husband John received unlimited guest passes to Disneyland and Universal Studios. NFL coaches receive yearly clothing and merchandise allowances. Some players have individual sponsorship deals with apparel companies. Numerous teams offer their personnel gratis movie admission, no-cost gym memberships, free golf memberships, and restaurant discounts. Some coaches and players receive a different dealer-issued car to drive every season. Perks vary by team, and their number and quality usually coincide with the team's win/loss record. Everyone wants to be with a winner.

"Free condo ski life tickets, a dealer car, and discounts on jewelry" are some of the team-sponsored perks that Pat Kennan says they've received, while Julianne Player says their perks have been somewhat more modest: "Occasionally, we can get tickets to basketball games or other events that are going on in the community. For us the freebies are usually tickets to community events."

For some, team-sanctioned perks are just the start. Using their partners' fame, some NFL women have a virtual rolodex of hookups. They talk about dropping the "Eagle bomb" or the "Forty-Niner bomb" during conversations with merchants in hopes of getting a lower price. Game tickets or signed photos can be exchanged for price cuts on roof re-shingling or sod installation.

The more a woman looks like the stereotypical "NFL wife"—wearing expensive jewelry, driving a flashy car, and not hiding an ample cleavage—often the bigger her discount. First-class upgrades are much harder to pull off in sweats and a greasy ponytail. Some women become so accustomed to special treatment that they become upset if they have to pay full price.

Informal and unsolicited NFL perks can be great, but it's rare if the person offering the discount wants only to be nice. Some NFL wives talked about how they learned this the hard way—how by accepting offers, they placed themselves in the donor's debt. One coach's wife described a building contractor who did her a "favor," and then three weeks later he called wanting four tickets to the Super Bowl.

Rosemary Bennett, the wife of a veteran punter, says she has learned to turn people down: "You've got to pay for it somewhere along the line—tickets to a game, a hat, or T-shirts. At first you think, 'Oh, he likes me.' But after a while you learn that you're going to pay for it somehow. I'm older, wiser, and a bit more leery."

Kim Ruddy says she has experienced her NFL connection working in reverse: "It can actually hurt you. People know that you play in the NFL, and they know you make money. Merchants think, 'I'll just charge them 10 percent more because of who they are,' rather than, 'I'll just take 10 percent off.' I think merchants want to up the price more often than take it away. I don't think anybody just hands things over to you."

Another veteran wife has also learned not to accept any offer at face value. She says, "I make people say clearly up front, 'I will give you this, but in return I want this.' And you should get it in writing. There are some people that are genuinely doing nice things for you because they like you and because they think it's neat. But in the beginning, it is really hard to tell them apart."

Ultimately, there is a wide discrepancy in how people in the NFL handle their money, just like anywhere. However, one player's wife seemed to sum up the perspective that many wives—and their player or coach husbands—reach eventually, if they get the chance. This woman's husband is not a starter, and he has to fight year to year for his job. In other words, he is typical of most players in the league, and the same can be said for his wife's opinions and perspective. She says:

It's not how people portray it. They believe that you're rolling in all this money. When you get into the league, you realize it depends on your contract. There are different levels in the league. I think anyone in the league is blessed, but not everyone is getting paid those large figures. Some can live that off-the-edge lifestyle and some really cannot, but they try to anyway. The rest of us are saving because we know this won't last a long time.

Before we got married, I knew my husband was not a very extravagant person, so I never really had high expectations like that. I always knew we would be taken care of comfortably but not extravagantly, comfortable but not crazy. For many women, I also think it's a part of marrying and getting older and maturing and understanding the view of the future. I think you start to realize the depth of the responsibility of [player's or coach's] career and the money that he brings in. You start to realize the burden that you take on.

9 NFL Beatings and Cheatings

Sports writers, ESPN producers, league representatives, many fans, and the public have strong opinions and beliefs regarding infidelity and domestic violence within the NFL, and their opinions tend to be sharply divided. When it comes to domestic abuse, one camp thinks the violent nature of the game, combined with the invincible "above the law" attitude exhibited by NFL men, means they are more likely than men outside of professional football to batter their wives and girlfriends. The other camp asserts that media portrayals and the extensive press coverage of high-profile players simply make it *seem* as though they are more prone to crimes of interpersonal violence.

As for infidelity, much of the public's opinion is influenced by Hollywood movies, which continue to sexualize the adoring female football fan. This leads the public to believe that there aren't any professional football players, married or single, who are immune to the irresistible "you-must-have-sex-with-me-now" allure of groupies.

Casting preexisting notions aside, I sought the stories and opinions of the people most closely and intimately involved in these situations, NFL women. Indeed, the some-times powerful and horrendous first-person accounts of beatings and cheatings at the hands of NFL husbands, boyfriends, and lovers left me shocked, angered, and saddened. The following excerpts are a sample of what I heard:

He has pulled and/or cut my hair off at times, and he discon-
nected the natural gas and electricity to my house when I filed
for a separation. He also stabbed me once, but that never made
the news.

He lied and said he was going to a basketball game . . . , but
when he left, the game was already over. He even checked into
a hotel so he could change into his party clothes. He didn't
want me to know anything about this party. Granted, it was all
over the radio. The station was promoting it for the players, so
of course it was going to bring in hundreds of groupies. I am
not stupid.

We will go back and forth because I don't let him talk to me
any sort of way. If he says something to me, I'll say something
back. But in this last incident a couple weeks ago . . . he pushed
me, then he kicked us out of the apartment. He was arrested
for assault and battery . . . but he really didn't do anything.
Granted, he shouldn't put his hand on me in any way. It was
all witnessed in front of my son, so now there are Children's
Services involved.

It's not like I'm scared of him or that he frightens me. But
verbally, he is extremely abusive. I know with his last girlfriend,
he told her that if she ever had him arrested, he would kill her.
Knowing him the way that I know him, I could tell that he was
hitting her. I could just tell.

Having studied violence against women as part of my master's
degree, I know that no matter who a woman is or what her partner
does for a living, traumatic experiences such as these can have a
tremendously negative impact on her psyche. In these situations,
the wife or girlfriend often feels ashamed, and she will frequently
blame herself, either entirely or in part. This applies to NFL women
as well. It is common for a depressed, downtrodden wife to respond
to attacks by thinking, "I deserved to get hit" and "No one else will
want me." A typical response from a disheartened girlfriend who
finds that her boyfriend has been cheating is to say, "He doesn't

think I'm sexy or beautiful anymore," and she will compare her body negatively to other, younger women. Since NFL women are frequently judged and evaluated on their physical beauty and appearance, infidelity can be particularly devastating to an NFL woman's self-esteem.

Regardless, not every woman to whom I spoke had a story to tell, and not all of those who did blamed the NFL. All NFL women recognize the temptations of celebrity and wealth in general, but most of those to whom I spoke did not think that being employed by professional football in and of itself led NFL men to act badly. In fact, some felt that NFL men were unfairly criticized and that problems of violence and abuse in the NFL were exaggerated; they thought football players and coaches were no more likely to be unfaithful or engage in domestic violence than men in any other profession. Despite their sometimes firsthand, personal experiences, these women said these issues were first and foremost society-wide problems, not NFL problems.

There are certainly unwholesome subcultures in the NFL that probably allow certain men to stray sexually or feel freer to be abusive. However, it is far too simplistic to say that playing the sport is the sole cause. For too long, U.S. society has tried to ignore these issues, which affect women everywhere. Seeking to blame them on a sport, or on one type of individual, can become just one more way of avoiding them.

Sirens on the Sidelines

The oversexualized, adoring female football fan is a staple of popular culture. Like the ever-present microphone-wielding sports reporters, they appear at the edges of the frame, a bevy of attractive, scantily clad young women squealing and waving at the gridiron warriors. They are portrayed as aggressive and starstruck, obsessively pursuing their favorite sports celebrity, often going to great lengths to entice him into bed. To the public they appear to be a near-constant invitation to have sex, one that no red-blooded male could resist, and because of them, many people assume that every NFL man must cheat on his wife. If his wife doesn't realize this, she must be incredibly naïve.

In fact, every NFL football team attracts female groupies, but do women agree with these outsider opinions about them? Do NFL women consider these female football enthusiasts to be a problem in the NFL? What about in their personal relationships? Would coaches use their NFL connection for sexual hook-ups as well? Do these lower-profile, lower-income men even have female admirers?

What happens when NFL women discover an affair? Do they ignore the matter, perhaps because they don't want to jeopardize their prestigious way of life? Or would they acknowledge the indiscretion but then quickly forgive him? The answers women gave were surprisingly varied.

Upon being asked any question related to groupies, several women—typically the younger, less experienced NFL wives—became clearly uncomfortable and quickly changed the topic. Such a reaction made me believe that they had indeed had experience with husbands' extramarital affairs and that the subject was just too painful to discuss.

One running back's wife recalled spending the first couple of years of her marriage constantly analyzing her relationship. She says, "You hear so many rumors [about NFL men and cheating], and you hear so many things. Who do you believe? What do you believe? Is that going to be me divorced five years from now? You start to wonder. I think it caused a lot more stress in our relationship."

One player's wife admitted that "wives are measured constantly. There is always an underlying current of, 'Everyone is after my husband.' It is just there. These women [groupies] want the experience. They don't want your husband; they want the experience. You just have to be one up against the competition. Especially if there is not a lot of substance to him, you need to stay one up on the competition."

Another NFL wife says, "You know what the sad thing is? A lot of his fans don't even want to know you exist. The young, good-looking things are in denial that he is married or has a girlfriend. He is their fantasy." Other wives and girlfriends reacted to these oft-repeated questions about the league's ready-and-willing female fans by sighing deeply and then stating that they did not find groupies bothersome in the least.

One player's wife says, "They can wear the makeup and be as cute as they want to be and wear the type of clothes they want.

It doesn't affect my life at all. I'm fine with them. But do I want them speaking to my husband on a first-name basis? No, I don't." Saying nearly the same thing, but speaking as if to the groupies, was another player's wife: "You can do all that prancing, but he's going to walk right past you and take his three kids and me and go home—so you're wasting your time."

Another player's wife says, "I am a big fan of women. I've always had a lot of women friends. I was not one of those women who just hung out with men. But it blows my mind when they just stare at him like I'm not there and I don't matter." On the other hand, she says, for the most part, "They have been really respectful when I am around at fan signings and things like that. Girls just look a little bummed when I walk into the room."

These NFL women also claimed that "male groupies" were much more likely to pursue their husbands and boyfriends than sexy female fanatics. These men and boys—with Sharpie pen in one hand and a football or some other item to be autographed in the other—wait in parking lots or outside restaurants for the fleeting chance to speak to or shake the hand of their beloved player. Cordoned off by ropes, they stand in the hotel lobby, then rush to the elevator for a chance to ride up with their idol. According to this group of NFL women, male football diehards outnumber women at least ten to one. One veteran player's wife says, "The people that I see as groupies are the goofy men all dressed up wearing the team outfits."

Still, not one NFL woman denied that certain female fans willingly made themselves available to football players, thus providing players with more opportunities for affairs than other men. Unlike most men, these recognizable and assumed-to-be-rich NFL men do not have to offer drinks, act charming, or even be nice to get these women to socialize with them.

Typically in their twenties and always primped and primed to look their sexiest, female groupies can be found every place NFL teams congregate, such as in bars, at player appearances, and at autograph signings. Though wives and families rarely travel to away games, nearly every woman with whom I spoke knew that groupies were a presence "on the road."

One player's wife says, "They usually want somebody to spend a lot of money on them. They usually want to use somebody that has money. I've seen some girls just waiting, and they'll do just about anything to get attention. When we're gone on away games, they will be hanging around outside the hotels, and it really turns me off. I feel sorry for them a little also, because I think that is all they know. I kind of ignore them."

Smart and aggressive, these groupies investigate beforehand when a team is scheduled to arrive from the airport. Discovering when teams have time off, some women will follow the players' taxis to local movie theaters or shopping malls. After an "inadvertent" meeting, the women will carefully script their introductions. "Oh, wow, the Panthers are in town this weekend? I just love football. Do you know how I could get tickets?"

Some players, particularly younger ones, hungrily lap up the attention of any attractive female in sight. True to the stereotype, these "American heroes" often have an oversized opinion of themselves, and they are quite eager to transfer the excitement of the playing field to the bedroom. The NFL sponsors a rookie symposium that discusses the dangers of casual, unprotected sex, but it can be hard for young men in their early twenties to visualize what it would mean to contract a deadly disease like AIDS when they are faced with such a female banquet.

Nor are players the only ones who get such attention from groupies. Coaches and other NFL personnel are not above taking advantage of their lofty positions to gain sex from easily impressed women. A highly recognizable head coach, particularly if he is charismatic and good looking, will have female admirers. And if there are no players in sight, some women who are attracted to the football world have been known to flirt with assistant coaches. Of course, coaches with their long work hours have fewer opportunities for sexual liaisons—but where there is a will, there is a lay.

Another popular venue for groupies is a team's private parking lot after games. Clusters of groupies congregate, or attempt to get into, these families-only restricted areas. A veteran player's wife describes the situation as follows:

We have what is called the Bimbo Squad. It is a group of girls at every game. A few of them change every year. About every four years you get a whole new squad. They come to the games dressed in practically nothing. I'm not sure how they get into our parking lot, but they do.

They wear their short shorts with their booties hanging out and everything else they've got going for them. They have nice bodies, and they're strutting their stuff. They think they're better looking than you are, and they are trying to get what you have.

They try to pick up anything that will look their way. They don't care if players are married or not. If players are looking at them, these girls are talking to them. We have had a couple of good, decent guys on our team actually hook up with these girls. Someone asked one of these players why he hooks up with these groupies, and he said, "It's just a place to take a piss."

Such attitudes are appalling, and one would like to think they are rare, but this is indicative of how some players regard groupies. Why would any woman put up with that? NFL women sometimes have a hard time understanding the motives of female groupies. Some of them are surely hoping to marry a mega-rich athlete, but some seem interested merely in saying they made some sort of connection or even had sex with a favorite player. Though it's extremely rare, some do have more sinister intentions: one player's wife relayed a story in which a groupie had sex with a player and stashed the used condom in her purse. She planned to reinsert the sperm, get pregnant, and then extract large child care payments from the father.

When athletes assume that every woman who shows interest in them also wants to have sex, it's not uncommon for charges of rape to follow after them. According to an article in *Newsweek* ("Kobe Off the Court," October 3, 2003), some NBA players instruct bodyguards to interview their potential bed partners. To avoid miscommunication and possible charges of sexual assault later, the bodyguards detail the player's exact sexual expectations. If a woman exhibits any qualms or indecision, the player cuts her loose and moves on to more willing participants. It's not hard to imagine that certain football players adopt this same strategy.

When the "Playa's" Moves Go Off the Field

If a player or coach is single, his sexual partners are nobody else's business. But if he has a girlfriend or wife, does that mean he is automatically inoculated against the allure and temptations of female groupies? Certainly not. Yet despite everything I've described so far, most of the women I queried dismissed the notion that groupies and infidelity were a concern in their personal relationships. However, these same women thought that groupies could be a problem for other NFL couples.

A young player's wife gave a telling response. "I would not have picked an NFL man for myself to marry," she said. Then after several thoughtful moments she added, "But I bet we all feel differently about our own husbands."

The majority of NFL women with whom I spoke were reluctant to rank the NFL "cheating average" higher than that for men outside of football. A lot of women were certain that the media had overstated the number of NFL men who engaged in sexual liaisons with groupies. Many of their comments were in line with the following statements I heard:

> If a man is not happy or satisfied at home, he is going to look for it whether he is in the NFL or not.

> I'm sure there are men in the NFL who do it, but I don't think that because they play in the NFL, it's going to cause them to cheat on their wives.

> I'd have the same concern about him going off with another woman if he were in the NFL as if he weren't.

The repercussions of a high-profile player's getting caught were yet another reason women thought their cheating averages would not be higher than for men in other fields. According to a player's wife, "I think with a professional athlete, in general, it [cheating] might be easier because women are more present, but I don't know if the infidelity rate is higher than general because they also have more to lose."

Women also said they didn't think players were running around more than other men because they "didn't hear about it too much." This comment was not surprising. Through my research and NFL experience, I've become privy to an unspoken rule among NFL men. Members on the same team *do not* tell their significant others about a cheating teammate. According to one anonymous NFL coach with whom I share a bathroom medicine cabinet, "If guys do talk, it will get out, and then it will cause problems." Case in point: one football player whose wife I befriended slept with a groupie just weeks after his wedding day, but it was several years later—and after the wife and I were no longer friends—before John told me about the indiscretion.

Some athletes have been known to keep two cell phones: one is for their wives, and the other is a private line for other women to call. When these "secret" cell phones are discovered, the numbers called usually correspond to cities on a team's away game schedule. Football players have only eight away games each season—compared to eighty or so road games per season in professional basketball and baseball—but this limited number of trips away from home may not necessarily equate to proportionally fewer affairs.

When it comes to the level of cheating in the NFL, some women may in fact be in denial. They don't want to know, and so they don't. However, as we have seen, NFL women are well aware of what can happen, and most are attuned to the signs of infidelity in their boyfriends or husbands.

Hell Hath No Fury

Studies have shown that arguments over extramarital affairs are a frequent precursor to domestic violence. The NFL women who spoke out about their abuse supported this claim. Their most physically violent confrontations with their partners began with quarreling over his cheating ways. As would be expected, some NFL men, particularly those with royalty-sized egos, do not like to be confronted with their wrongdoings.

Like scorned lovers everywhere, most NFL women respond to news of an infidelity with anger, rage, and sometimes a desire for revenge. Given the public nature of an NFL woman's life—her husband and family will be known to the league, often to an entire city, and sometimes to the country—the potential for embarrassment and humiliation is enormous. There is no setting in which she can hide, for in every area of her life she is identified with her husband. And as we have seen, she is often the last to know. Her husband's or boyfriend's teammates, and perhaps a good portion of the league, will have heard about her husband's infidelities long before she does.

As one famous player's wife admitted somewhat wryly, any argument between high-profile spouses will be noticed, whatever the source of the conflict: "Being that he is a public figure, where everything we do is under a microscope, sometimes it doesn't allow us to have major, major blowups . . . [as one] would probably like to."

An NFL woman's anger and resentment over an infidelity can be immense, but according to most women with whom I spoke, it was unusual for NFL women to take revenge with affairs of their own. The reason may have less to do with the women than with their partners. As one wife says, "What man would want to sleep with a football player's wife? I don't know. That is a pretty big guy to have on your butt." Several NFL women stated that they found it difficult to have even simple friendships with men because many men are intimidated by their football-player husbands. However, some women said that wives do have affairs. Many NFL women *are* beautiful, and they are home alone as often as their partners are on the road. It is quite easy to engage in a little payback sex. I was told of one situation in which an NFL wife did this by having an affair with her husband's teammate.

The main concern once an infidelity is discovered, however, is not how to exact revenge, but whether to stay in the relationship or not. For many, Vanessa Bryant represents one situation in which NFL wives can see themselves.

In 2003, a woman charged Vanessa's husband, Los Angeles Lakers' basketball star Kobe Bryant, with sexual assault. Bryant denied the charges of rape, but he admitted that he had sex with the woman. Despite her husband's adultery, Vanessa sat next to Bryant during the nationwide press conference in which he admitted what he'd done. As her husband spoke, Vanessa looked at him adoringly, held his hand, and even mouthed the words, "Are you okay?"

The majority of the NFL women with whom I spoke said they were shocked and taken aback by Vanessa's behavior. They would not want to be in the same country, let alone in the same room, as their husbands at that point. Everything about Vanessa's behavior indicated that she believed her husband was innocent of the criminal charges and that she had already forgiven him for breaking his wedding vows.

I do not know what Vanessa really thought. However, some of the NFL women said that she was acting like NFL women they knew—women who had been married young (Vanessa was a teenage bride) to men who went on to become rich and famous. Such a woman had never gathered the necessary life skills or self-confidence to consider demanding a divorce and facing life on her own. Her entire identity was as this man's wife, and putting up with his infidelity was less frightening than imagining life without him.

The wife of a famous player put this fear very succinctly: "When your husband is out there in the public eye, I just feel like the stakes are a little bit higher for him to know that he is the most important thing in your life—because somebody may be waiting in the wings. That is not my motivation for it, but you have seen the casualties. There is somebody waiting who would make him the most important thing."

Many women acknowledged that the extent of a man's crime had to be weighed against the life they'd built together and all that would be lost if they pressed for divorce. Some women also plainly get attached to a material lifestyle. One retired player's wife says, "At first, some women might say they are getting out, but then they imagine another woman stepping in and taking what they've got, and then they change their minds. They figure, 'I put all this work into getting us here. Ain't nobody else gonna take my place.'"

One player's wife reacted strongly to this idea. She says, "I don't care if my husband scores the winning touchdown of the Super Bowl. I will not sit back and watch him do things detrimental to our marriage and family. I would give back all my cars, jewels, and trips to have a happy home with a husband who wants to be with me and our kids instead of a twenty-year-old groupie-stripper."

It Comes Down to the Man

According to numerous veteran NFL women, the responsibility for philandering husbands falls squarely on the shoulder pads of the philandering husbands. The availability and eagerness of some female fans shouldn't matter. These women maintain that groupies are only a problem if NFL men allow them to be and that the league's truly good and decent guys don't give groupies a second glance.

A veteran player's wife states, "I truly believe it is all in the way that the man carries himself. Don't get me wrong; I know that some women can be aggressive—my husband was mailed pictures and videos from interested women before we were married—but if players make it known they are committed to their wives, groupies tend to go after and cling more to the ones who are not married."

Or as one NFL wife says, "The faithful men I know don't seem to linger and hang out after games or team events and say, 'Who is this, and who is that?' referring to other women."

NFL wives believe that men who engage in sex with groupies are basically immature. One coach's wife says sharply, "These men are insecure little boys who need attention." The mature men realize that the women fawning over them care only about their public persona. These women lust after the uniform or the bank account or the fame. Simply put, if NFL men are the toughest of the tough, if they can discipline themselves to withstand incredible amounts of physical strain and mental pressure, it seems that they can find the strength to keep their jockstraps securely fastened for a weekend away from home. In any case, it doesn't take long before many of these young men start to question the "glory of fame" and begin to put their fans' adulation in perspective.

One player's wife says, "The smart guys know that this is all the land of make-believe. They know the reasons those types of women come after them. Those women don't know the real person . . . not like I do."

Football's True Warriors: Survivors of Domestic Violence

NFL football is a violent game, and many assume that it requires violent men to play it, men who may not always be able to control their rage. Since the focus of NFL domestic violence is primarily on the men who are suited up and on the field, as opposed to their coaches, my questions were directed toward the wives and girlfriends of players. However, I do not mean to imply that professional coaches do not engage in domestic violence; it is just that coaches were not the focus of this research.

A startling number of the women who had experienced physical abuse in their NFL relationships wanted to go on the record. Unabashed and undeterred, the divorced wife of a player said, "I have no shame. I have no image to uphold, and I will speak my truth."

However, for several reasons I chose to protect their identities, even when some women said they wanted their names to be published. Most crucially, few of the men who will be discussed were ever arrested for their assaults. In addition, charges of domestic violence are potentially career-damaging—even if, from a historical perspective, such charges rarely seem to threaten NFL jobs. Though I do not doubt the women to whom I spoke, bringing these charges to court is the only fair way to determine if they're true. Finally, I feared for the women themselves. These types of men, after having their transgressions aired publicly, would not be above retribution. As I write this, I am keenly aware that silence because of the fear of retaliation helps keep the cycle of violence intact.

Of course, my heart raced and my fists clenched upon hearing the terrible evils committed upon my NFL sisters. Even more appalling, however, is that throughout the United States similar horrific tales are tragically commonplace. According to the U.S. Department of Justice, a woman is beaten in the United States every nine seconds. Domestic violence is an insidious crime that crosses all social, economic, and racial lines, and it is the leading cause of injury to women. My indignity and outrage extend to every one of these women.

My objective in this book is to address narrower but more common questions. Does domestic violence occur more often in NFL families than in nonfootball families, and, if so, what are the reasons?

I discovered that the majority of NFL women *disagreed* with the prevailing attitude that football players were more prone to physically abusing their partners than men outside of football. The women who acknowledged that domestic violence was an issue in their relationships (either through an in-person interview or an anonymous survey) were very few—maybe 10 percent.

For the most part, NFL women felt it came down to the old adage that sex and violence sell, particularly when the stories are about well-known people. It is considered more "newsworthy" when an NFL woman gets smacked around than when the neighborhood soccer mom is routinely covered with bruises. The majority of the women with whom I spoke believed the media overreported incidents of NFL domestic violence and that the image of physically abusive football players was an overstated generalization.

One well-known player's wife says, "People are putting a stigma on the NFL. Domestic violence is happening with men every day, whether they are in the NFL or they work at a bank or they are lawyers or police officers. Why are people choosing to say that NFL guys are so corrupt?"

Kim Ruddy says, "I don't think you hear about Joe Blow next door beating up his wife as much as you would about a guy in the limelight. You're just reading about it a lot more. If you're in the public eye, it's going to be public knowledge. It's not everybody. It's just a few guys here and there. Everybody is human, and just because they're athletes and play professional football, it doesn't make them subhuman. It doesn't make them come from another planet. Everybody has emotions, and everybody has problems. How do you know what really went on behind those closed doors anyway?"

Or as another player's wife says, "It's called taking off your pads and your helmet, which to me is just that simple. It's never been an issue. When he comes out, he knows he's Daddy and a husband and no longer a player."

Can You Blame It on the Game?
But what about the game's inherent violence, some ask. Supporters of the theory that football players are more violent believe that NFL men cannot separate the rough-and-tough aspects of their job from their behavior off the field. Why wouldn't players use brute physical force at home to achieve their goals since these tactics work well on the field?

In fact, some NFL women believe the game probably does make players more prone to domestic violence, though the inherent violence of the game itself is only one part of the equation. Fame-inflated egos and drugs play their parts, too. As one woman says, "For sixty minutes they're told to go hit, and they're paid to do it, and they are supposed to turn it off when they go home, win, lose, or draw. When a wife wants to say, 'Honey, would you please do this?' then it's like, pow. 'Look, you, I'm the big celebrity. Why are you asking me to pick up the dishes?'"

A coach's wife speculates, "They used to say it had a lot to do with steroid use, but now supposedly that is not happening. I think players overall have to be more aggressive. With that type of personality, I think, if they can't handle it themselves, then yes, they do take it out on their wives or maybe their children."

Kim Singletary doesn't single out NFL players as any more abusive than others, but she says, "In the cases of the ones I have seen that were abusive during their careers, a lot of the time, the abuse was substance enhanced. To me, it's like the RPMs are running a little too high. They cannot control themselves."

Other NFL wives rebutted this notion of hyper-violent NFL men by presenting their own player-husbands as examples. Of her husband, one wife says, "I think he has a tremendous love of the game, which means he is extremely competitive." She didn't, however, think this meant he was inherently violent or aggressive—two attributes he never displays off the field. "My mother asked me, 'How can he be so gentle and mild at home? He plays such a violent sport.' Yes, but his job is to protect the quarterback. Sure, he is very competitive, but it is more in a protective way."

Kim Ruddy says, "If there is any aggression, it comes out on the field. I've never seen in my home even a raised voice, let alone a raised hand. People have misconceptions of big men, that they're violent. I have a very large man, and let me tell you, he is a gentle giant. He's never raised his voice to my kids or myself in the nine years that we've been together."

Another argument holds that rather than the physical violence of the game, it is the tremendous stress and pressures of professional football that some players cannot handle. In this scenario, players have outbursts at home as a release for their workplace tension. No doubt football is an extremely stressful occupation—every Sunday players must excel or worry about being demoted or even cut.

But this is true of many jobs, particularly in a recession or a bad economy.

In this case, several women with whom I spoke believed that football actually helped their husbands release any pent-up stress or emotional tension that came with the job. These women said that the sport itself acted as a channel to expel violent behaviors. Exhausted and banged up, these men do not have the energy to fly into wild rages at home. "Everyone knows that doing something physical helps get rid of your anger," said one player's girlfriend.

Kim Ruddy agrees: "I don't see why they wouldn't be able to leave it on the field. I think it's easier for those guys. They lift weights every day. They get to go out for three hours and beat up some other three-hundred-pound guy. Go to the gym or hit a dummy for three hours, and see how aggressive you feel."

Too Famous for Their Own Good

Being famous in itself does not lead a person to commit domestic violence, but if a person is already prone to act violently, being famous clearly provides an inflated sense of privilege that makes it easier for the person to justify his actions. NFL women agreed that today's athletes sometimes feel—and not without evidence—that the laws don't always apply to them. An abuser in the NFL does not have to think as hard about the consequences of his actions if he's caught.

In his book about the NFL, *Bloody Sundays*, Mike Freeman writes: "Players are no longer afraid of repercussions, from either the courts or the NFL. They know a physical attack on a wife or girlfriend will probably fail to lead to a prison term because the woman, as often happens in domestic violence cases, many not seek to prosecute her attacker . . . . Even if the abused woman does not refuse to testify, most players are wealthy enough to hire a top-notch attorney who can work the system to keep them free."

Freeman continues: "Players, especially the highly talented ones, also understand that no matter what they do, short of a murder conviction, there will always be a job waiting for them in football. They've learned. They have watched this scenario play itself out a hundred times. . . . Teams and the court system make embarrassing compromises so a player can take the field despite accusations of abuse."

The sports media must share part of the blame for this privileged "you-can't-touch-me" attitude among professional athletes, since the media habitually discredit women's stories of abuse. When these stories arise, wives are treated with suspicion, while the players are allowed to remain heroes.

Even judges and police officers have been known to give preferential treatment to sports stars. One NFL woman recalled an incident in which she had been beaten by her husband and the police arrived at her house to take a statement. As she detailed the specifics of her assault, the male officers suddenly asked what college her husband attended, then how much money he made.

With exasperation, she says, "As if my nose wasn't dripping blood right in front of them."

This insensitivity from law enforcement, combined with the fact that everyone will read about what happened in the following day's newspaper, prevents many NFL women from even calling the police.

Several wives agreed with this, but said it could cut both ways. One said, "If you're spiteful and you want to get him, you can really get him. So it would be either protect your husband and not report it, or it would be, yes, I'll get you. A woman could really damage his reputation and maybe his career."

Another NFL woman supported this, saying, "I think if women want to be in the public more, this would be their way of getting their name in." However, she concluded, "I think other women, though, wouldn't say a word. It would be hush, hush, leave it out. They don't even tell their friends what happened because they don't want to have any attention drawn to themselves at all."

Family History Trumps Occupation

Most of the NFL women with whom I spoke, including those who had been abused, thought that a player's family background, not his occupation, had the greatest influence on his tendency toward domestic violence. If he was taught as a child that hitting and punching were acceptable ways to deal with problems, he continued this behavior as an adult.

As Kim Singletary says, "The root of it to me is broken homes.

We have created a society of rage-filled kids. I don't even know if they know where the rage is coming from, but everybody has this rage."

She continues, "You have got an aggressive child, and the football coach wants him. It is sort of like a Band-Aid on a cancer. For all the years he has played, this has been his outlet. No one has addressed this issue. As soon as he is done playing, at whatever point in his career it is, there is no more outlet. The woman in your life, or the people in your life are now the outlet."

NFL women also believed that a man's maturity level was a better indicator of whether he'd be abusive at home than his job or celebrity status. According to a veteran player's wife, "Players can turn violence off by being mature. Maturity helps them separate the game from real life."

Wanted: Football Skills and Good Character

Though most of the women with whom I spoke did not believe that NFL men were more likely than other men to abuse their partners or engage in extramarital affairs, it is important to note that most of these women were either married or in long-term relationships. My research did not target casual girlfriends and/or sex partners, former wives (for instance, those who may have left their relationships because of violence or affairs), or NFL "baby mommas"—women who had mothered a player's child but remained unmarried to the father (for a number of reasons).

In fact, as I look back on my conversations with unmarried women, many of their comments seemed to suggest that they had experienced a disproportionate amount of gender violence and unfaithfulness in their relationships with NFL men. It could be that NFL men do not give these women the same respect they would accord a wife. Or perhaps, since these unmarried women were typically younger than the married women, their sense of self and personal identity were less established. If so, it's possible that they were still somewhat intimidated by NFL celebrity and as a result more accepting of a player's appalling behavior. More research is needed with this group of women before any conclusions can be drawn.

Even if it is true that NFL men are not any more likely to be physically abusive to the opposite sex, however, the league needs to permanently sack any player who cannot control himself off the field. It is a disgusting but undeniable fact that too many NFL teams care only about how a player performs on the field and not about his behavior off of it, even when that behavior becomes criminal. Instead of team owners taking a stand, time and time again teams sign or retain players after criminal charges of domestic violence have been made against them.

Several years ago, after the game's public image began taking a beating, the league finally stepped in with an antiviolence policy. The plan, implemented in 1997, requires that any player accused of a violent crime submit to counseling. If a player refuses the team's counseling, he can be fined or suspended. A conviction for a violent crime can result in a suspension, and a second conviction can result in a player's being banned from the game.

This policy sounds good. But I question the effectiveness of such counseling. What, if anything, motivates teams to work for a positive change in their players? How do teams measure the effects of this counseling? When allegations of domestic violence arise against a player, the standard public relations response is "We are looking into these allegations, and we will take the appropriate measures." This comes off as nothing more than lip service, and this nonresponse by teams is probably the most credible evidence supporting the claim that players have a higher likelihood of committing domestic violence: if the owner or team doesn't care and if the paycheck is not going to stop, then why should the player?

The league's antiviolence plan needs to be bulked up. Some suggest a year's ban for a first offense and a permanent ban for a second offense. If team personnel have a difficult time envisioning how their squad would perform without their star abuser, perhaps the men in charge should instead imagine him beating up their own daughters or sisters or wives. I would ask them to replay this mental tape for a few moments, then take a stand against gender violence.

Turn Out the Lights, the Party's Over **10**

When Deems May played tight end in the NFL, he would shake his head as he watched his wife, Susan, prepare for work in the mornings. Though she took a leave of absence during the season, in the off-season Susan worked full-time as a real estate agent. Susan says she preferred working because "I had a college degree and I felt I needed to work. I have always liked being very busy, and I also knew that football was not going to last forever."

Every morning in the off-season, the moment her feet hit the floor, Susan would power up her computer and scan the new home listings that had appeared overnight. Next, she would take a series of phone calls from typically stressed-out clients, who might be frantic over a sub-par inspection report or furious at a holdup by their loan institution. While one hand applied eye makeup, the other scribbled on escrow forms. The same hectic, demanding pace continued for the rest of the day.

"Even though I only worked in my job from December to August, I never took it lightly," Susan recalls.

Deems was always supportive of Susan's career, but he still would wonder why she went to the trouble. Now retired from the NFL, Deems has begun a second career as a financial adviser, and according to Susan, his new job has made him see things differently. She says, "It is a huge wake-up call, going into the real world. It made my husband really appreciate what I did. He used to think that I worked so hard for so little money. Now he understands that is what most people do."

Deems played tight end for the San Diego Chargers for six years, and then spent another three seasons blocking and catching for the Seattle Seahawks. During this time, he had no qualms about living large. The couple enjoyed hosting large-scale parties, complete with private bands, and for a while they even rented an ocean-front condo near San Diego. "That cost us a fortune," Susan remembers.

The football player enjoyed lavishing luxurious gifts on his wife—Chanel earrings, purple label Ralph Lauren, and spectacular Versace garments—as well as being generous with his family. He offered gifts of Rolex watches and treated his mother-in-law with Fendi handbags.

When she was growing up, Susan and her family took modest vacations and drove unassuming cars, even though, as a doctor's family, they were relatively wealthy. Most of the families Susan knew back then were equally conservative with their money, and that was how she originally thought she and Deems should live. But it can be hard not to get caught up in the flashy, flamboyant side of the NFL. Susan says they simply "decided to relax and enjoy it while it lasted. My husband has always enjoyed giving extravagant gifts, and he takes pleasure in it." Then Susan asks, "How do you turn down a new Escada outfit when your husband was thrilled to death that he could buy it for you?"

Despite their extravagances, the couple tried to budget their expenses, but in hindsight, Susan confesses that they could have done better. She says, "Every time we were about to spend on something that we did not need, like buying $10,000 worth of watercraft every year, we should have invested. Most young couples are struggling when they first marry and don't have the extra money to invest, but we did."

Inescapably, whether he is a household name or a little-known rookie, an NFL player's decision to retire is most often involuntary; it is forced on him by management or by injuries. Deems May's professional exit was no exception. While scraping and dueling it out during his ninth sweaty summer training camp, the healthy veteran thought he would make the squad at least one more year.

The Seattle Seahawks, however, felt that a younger tight end could do the same job for less money, and they released Deems at the end of training camp.

Though Deems did not want to stop playing at that point—at least financially, Susan says, "we could always use a couple more years"—he decided it was time. Susan had recently given birth to the couple's first child, a daughter, and having the chance to spend time with her was a big consideration. Also, because he was released at the end of training camp, when most teams are set with their rosters, Deems didn't want, as Susan says, "to sit around and wait for someone to get hurt. He also did not want to go to a team and then be released weeks later."

Upon Deems's retirement, Susan says that her life "went on as usual." She continued working as a real estate agent, as she always had, and this made her transition into the nonfootball world much easier for her than it could be for women without already established careers. Susan now speaks of her NFL days and all the perks of that life with no longing or regrets. She says, "I enjoyed it, but I never lived for it."

Deems May, on the other hand, did not shift into nonfootball life nearly as smoothly. From the day they are cut, football players are often bombarded with questions about their future. Media, friends, and family all ask the same thing: "So what are you going to do next?" Since few football players have another career lined up—indeed, most expect to be employed by football at the moment they are suddenly "retired"—these probes can make them feel terribly uncomfortable and often inadequate. Coaches—particularly older men in the latter stages of their careers—can also be forced into retirement, and this same emotional dynamic can be true for them as well.

Deems was fortunate in that he had the perfect distraction for inquiring minds. When it came time for him to run errands in town, Susan says, "He had this little girl to tote around everywhere with him. People would say, 'Oh, look at this beautiful child.' And then they would talk about her. She became everyone's focus, including his."

Deems was able to step into a new role, one even bigger than that of football player. He became "Daddy." Yet despite the pleasure and the welcome distraction his daughter gave him, Deems needed time to grieve his loss. This is true for discarded athletes in any sport.

Susan says, "When he retired, he felt like I used to feel when we first got married and I did not have anything to do. We moved to a new city and state, across the country, and I did not know anyone. He was gone all day working, and you usually meet people through your work or children. No children and no work at age twenty-three. I was very lost. I completely understood how he felt."

It took a year for Deems to put his playing career to rest and find something new that interested him. During this time, Susan says, "I felt so bad for him. It may be easier for couples who do not have to make any career decisions right away because financially they are set. I am not sure; I wouldn't know about them. Deems never made multimillions."

Susan admits that she "was in a hurry" for him to get started in a new career, but not necessarily because the family needed the money; she says that by "living simply," they could get by. However, "I knew how long it took me to become successful. I knew that whatever he decided to do, it would take some time to do well. The sooner he started that, the better."

Deems decided he would become a financial adviser, and at his current firm he's in charge of client development. Susan says he chose the financial world because "he is fascinated by the stock market and investment tools. He also liked the flexibility in the career. He did not want a nine-to-five job. He does not like to sit behind a desk very long."

As Susan knew he would, in his new job Deems became a rookie again. Everyone else with whom he worked already had ten to twelve years of experience. In addition, Susan said her husband mistakenly assumed that his past teammates would become his clients: "Even though he may have blocked for them, it still does not mean that they will trust him with their money."

Susan says it took a couple of years for Deems to get comfortable with his NFL retirement and to find success in his new career. "We are now in our fourth year, and things are great. He is being offered different business opportunities. He is doing the radio pre- and post-game for the Carolina Tarheels. I will not say that football is out of his system, but *playing* football is out of his system."

In fact, compared to most players and their spouses, Susan and Deems have adjusted to post-NFL life quite smoothly and even happily. Susan says, "Deems and I still have to work, but we both love our jobs." Coaches experience some of the same emotions and issues upon retirement, but their circumstances are usually slightly different—most coaches are able to retire later in life and on their own terms. However, even when players or coaches make the decision themselves, it is always rough watching the sport to which they have given their lives continue to function just fine without them.

The Desire Remains

Even for the blessed few who leave the NFL on their own terms and are set for life financially, retirement is almost never an idyllic voyage into a golden sunset. These retired players or coaches and their spouses may indeed, as the popular fantasy holds, spend many of their days traveling, attending celebrity events and board meetings, and presiding over charities with their names on them. These couples no longer need to work another day in their lives, and some won't. They spent a long time in the league, guarded their income wisely, and have earned the opportunity to relax and enjoy themselves.

Very, very few NFL players or coaches enter retirement this way, but even for them, the competitive desire never leaves. In retirement, these men often become bored and restless rather than content. Pushed off the field and out of the cozy locker room, they don't know where they can turn to find the challenges and excitement that playing or coaching football once provided. They have always had a team. They have always been a part of something bigger than themselves. In the nonfootball world, ex-athletes frequently don't know where they fit in. A handful of well-known former players and coaches have enjoyed extended NFL careers in the broadcasting booth, but even many of them have admitted they would do just about anything for the chance to put on pads or step on the sidelines once again.

Players probably don't miss getting beaten to a bloody pulp week after week or having to endure another surgery; likewise, ex-coaches are thrilled to get more than four hours of sleep a night. But in my

experience and that of the wives to whom I spoke, countless numbers of retired NFL men say they miss the purpose and direction
that football gave them—or at the very least, that weekly adrenaline
rush.

Kim Singletary says that she and her husband Mike are happy to
be back in the league after ten years of NFL retirement:

> Last year was Mike's first year coaching. My sister has a very
> planned and orderly life, and there is a part of me that longs
> for that, especially during those days when I feel like a single
> mom. But I know I would never trade this for that. I would
> say there is a certain amount . . . of physical endorphins or
> something. There is a high, I think. You usually feel it in
> November. Everybody is dragging and exhausted, but there is
> something about that game that just keeps you going. There
> is some kind of chemical that you get out of it because "ordi-
> nary" just doesn't cut it anymore. After you have experienced
> it, every moment is at an extreme.

Wealthy former players like Mike Singletary—who can choose
not to work another day again or who get the opportunity to return
to the game in another capacity—are the fortunate ones! The great
majority of NFL players don't play long enough or save well enough
to make a retired life of leisure a reality. Many players are "retired"
before they're thirty, making a second income after football a financial necessity. Some find themselves pounding the pavement
looking for work mere months after cashing their last NFL paycheck; moreover, finding a job at all, much less a satisfying one,
can be surprisingly difficult. Though most have attended college,
the majority of NFL players have not earned their undergraduate
degrees. (According to the NFLPA, in 2003, 800-plus players out of
approximately 1,800 had their Bachelor's degrees.) Most have been
playing a *game* since childhood and lack other employable skills.
Football is all they know.

It is sad but true that some cash-strapped ex-gridiron stars are
reduced to taking jobs moving boxes in warehouses or walking
door-to-door selling household cleaners in order to put food on
their families' tables. In the end, no matter what they do, some

ex-players and ex-coaches simply cannot adjust. Maybe they hate their dull second careers, or they desperately miss the glory and fame that accompanied their playing days. Most were pushed out before they were ready, and they can't come to grips with their loss of status and identity. Others have been unable or unwilling to live within their newly reduced means and become overwhelmed by a mounting pile of bills. Suicide is rare, but tragically, a few NFL players have become so severely depressed during retirement that they have taken their own lives.

Jackie Rice says, "You see a lot of former players and talk to them, and they miss it. Some of the guys who are commentators now on TV came into the league the same time Jerry came into the league. They say, 'This guy is still playing, and I envy him. I wish I could still play competitively.' They miss it tremendously. They have played this sport all throughout college; some people got started in Pop Warner. Jerry got started in high school. This is something that they have basically done their whole lives."

Of her husband's retirement, one player's wife says, "I can tell that there is a bit of jealousy when there are players that were with him that are still playing, but he handles it much better. I think his pride is just taking a beating right now, especially since he knows that if he had managed his finances much better, it might not be so important that I worked. He has actually put in a few applications. I think he thought that it was going to be easy to jump right back in and get a job, but it hasn't been."

Another player's wife talked about how post-retirement depression affected her husband. "We were not communicating well. I had a baby and started a new job, and we moved. He wasn't very talkative, and he would say, 'I am not happy.' I would say, 'We just had a baby! What do you mean you are not happy?' "

At some point, nearly every retired player or coach wishes he could return to the game. For some, the feeling arrives in days; for others, it may take a couple of seasons without football to realize how much they miss it. Many men make their peace with this feeling and move on. However, some players, despite advancing age and debilitating injuries, stage desperate attempts at comebacks, while others try to return to the game as coaches or scouts or by joining a team's player personnel department. It is becoming almost common for veteran head coaches to retire for a year or two and then unretire at the first chance to helm a fledging team.

For some, the desire to return can become quite poignant. As one ex-player's wife said, "He always says he wished he had a second chance to make more money to make a difference. Also, having a son now and not being in the NFL anymore—not being able to share that with his son is really hard on him, too."

"Not What I Imagined"

It is nearly impossible for NFL women to escape their partners' emotional upheavals as they deal with retirement from the game. For months, if not years, the retiree will be a model of frustration, discontent, and sometimes bitterness.

"Hey!" these women think to themselves. "What happened? Retirement was not supposed to be like this."

Most of the NFL women to whom I spoke, if they weren't outright longing for retirement, at least imagined that it would bring with it a much needed rebalancing and refocusing of a couple's relationship. NFL women were happy to be done with the stress of game day, finished with the hassle of being the weekend activity director, and finally through with worrying about frisky female fans.

As Pat Kennan says, "I haven't missed our exit from the NFL at all. It provided us with a wonderful life for many years, but the lack of any job security whatsoever finally wore me out. I also hated seeing my husband work such long, horrendous hours and just look so tired most of the time. It was time to do something different."

Some NFL women imagine retirement will be a time of heavenly bliss spent with the man they love. At last, he won't be distracted when he is asked a question. He won't be too tired (or sore and bruised) to help around the house. Surely the enthusiasm and dedication he had for football will be redirected toward the relationship. Heck, after discovering everything he missed over the years and how much he loves being with his family, he might even apologize for all the time and energy he spent on the game. This is what some NFL women secretly fantasize.

Whether it's implicit or explicit, NFL women usually strike a bargain with the game. For however many years a spouse is in the NFL, women subvert their needs and desires to help him succeed.

In countless ways, they receive the message that "nothing is as important as winning the next game." Some NFL women believe this is literally true, but others understand that they have little choice but to act as if it were. If they love and want to stay with their boyfriends or husbands, they must learn to find happiness in second place.

Then, the "golden years" arrive, and the dream life that they've held out for themselves as the reward for all their sacrifices comes to resemble more of a nightmare. Oftentimes, in addition to dealing with their husbands' negative emotions, wives are forced to examine their own repressed issues. Years of frustration and buried resentment can rise to the surface.

One player's wife talked about the lack of patience she had for her husband's post-retirement struggles. She says, "I made the mistake of saying, 'Why is it such a big deal [to find another job]? We are doing fine.' My friends tell me that may have been worse than a punch in the stomach. He keeps saying that he wants to contribute, but I just don't want him taking a job just to have a job and not be happy and complain about it constantly."

Any rocky emotions can become intensified because now, for the first time in years, the couple is together all the time. There is no month-long break during summer training camp, no away-game weekends. One NFL wife described the first year after her husband's retirement as almost unbearable, and this was echoed by many women, who said the first year was always the hardest.

The wife said, "He would not get off the couch, and he was always in a bad mood. He didn't go to any of his former team's games—not that they ever invited him. To this day he doesn't watch any football on TV. Maybe it's terrible to say, but I was done being supportive. I was sick of it."

Coaches' wives in particular spend much of their partners' careers making the majority of the family and household decisions. In retirement, couples need to reset their interpersonal boundaries, even down to household chores like who folds the towels, who walks the dog, or who sweeps the leaves off the front porch.

When former Raiders' head coach Tom Flores retired, he and his wife Barbara made a conscious decision to reconnect. Barbara says, "Tom and I did errands together, and he called it 'Driving Miss Barbie.' He had never done things like that before. We did lots of fun things together. It's kind of like you are newly married again, and you are just discovering new things to do and enjoy. It takes an adjustment to a completely different way of life. Patience and understanding help."

Barbara continues, "Most coaches' wives have spent a lot of their married life without their husbands around. So when they are around all of the time, it kind of drives you crazy. I think that it is important that the ex-coach have some interest that will keep him occupied."

Tom sorely missed the excitement of coaching football, but Barbara says the former Super Bowl championship coach was able to "get his fix" by doing radio broadcasts of Raiders' games. Tom Flores was luckier than most NFL men. He was able to maintain his involvement in football even after his coaching days were over. Without these football ties, Barbara feels the couple probably would not have had as smooth a transition into retirement.

Barbara admits that they have been very fortunate. "Our relationship has changed. Retirement has been a time to become closer and to get to know each other again. I have really enjoyed that part—spending time together, enjoying each other and new experiences."

In truth, not every woman is happy to find her relationship changed. For women who, whether they realized it at the time or not, married their husbands in part for the financial rewards and exciting lifestyle the NFL offered, retirement can suddenly make their partners seem less attractive. Though none of the NFL women said this about themselves, they did say they had known other couples where this was true. When the NFL was gone, so was the wife or girlfriend, though this rarely applied to women who had been with their partners since high school or college. Kim Singletary makes the following observation:

> I have seen too many guys devastated by "Barbie." Her intentions start out good—he is my knight in shining armor, and I am going to stick with him—but when the rubber meets the road, it takes some substance to endure that life. When the glamour is gone—for too many couples, that was their foun-

dation. When she leaves him, usually he is retired or injured or out of the game, out of the glory.

I think if they met after he was playing football, at some point, when football is over, she has got to look at him and say, "Now, do I love him, this person? Do I love the dad that he his? Do I love the husband that he is?"

Nevertheless, according to the women with whom I spoke, if a couple breaks up after retirement, it is much more common for the ex-athlete to do the leaving. Almost stereotypically, he turns to someone younger and more attractive to supply the adoration and praise that are suddenly missing in his life.

Extreme Financial Makeover
Upon a husband's retirement, every NFL couple or family is faced with a similar issue: they must learn to get by with less. This is easier for some than for others, but for all it usually means some unexpected and sometimes uncomfortable adjustments. Spending habits are among the first things to change.

A few weeks after her cornerback husband retired, one wife recalls, "There was a very expensive pair of shoes I thought I wanted. But I was having an argument with myself over whether I should get them. I didn't need them; I just wanted them. I realized that I was upset because of the fact that I had to do that now. After your husband retires, you have to take a step back and ask yourself, 'Do I really need to pay that kind of money?'"

Kim Singletary remembers, "In his ninth or tenth year when he was playing, there was something in the back of your mind saying, you know, you really need to slow down the spending. This is not going to last. Then girlfriends of mine whose husbands had retired would say things like, 'You better get it now because you are not going to get it when he retires.' But you still think, oh, I probably will. You are in denial."

Denial regarding retirement, particularly among players, runs rampant. Preparation for a post-football future is hindered by their refusal to even imagine what their lives will be like once they leave the game. Their reaction is probably natural. Few people want to think about the day they can no longer perform their job, especially when it is a job they dearly love. It is too painful.

Many NFL women put on similar blinders. Time and time again, the women to whom I spoke stated that they never really thought about the money or the lifestyle coming to an end. Include Chandra Hollier, a medical doctor and retired NFL wife, as one of the nonbelievers. She says, "Even though Dwight played for nine years and I knew after three or four it was gravy, I just didn't even think about retirement. When he didn't get picked up by Miami, I was in shock."

Denial regarding finances can continue even after retirement, when, despite a greatly reduced income, some retired players foolishly keep spending money at the same, pre-retirement rate. These men continue to own several houses and pay multiple mortgages, buy whatever consumer goods they want, and consistently pick up the restaurant tabs for twenty of their closest friends.

Not that you need to be foolish or frivolous to go broke. Some former athletes, hoping to generate as much income as they can, take all their savings and invest them or start businesses with them, and sometimes these investments don't work out. Some unscrupulous business types even target former athletes with bogus investment deals, but bad luck and financial inexperience probably play just as big a role. According to one retired wife, "If you want to make big money, then you have to invest big money, and that is a bigger risk."

No More Mrs. Football Wife

Just as much as her husband, a woman can become lost after retirement from the NFL. Some women have been just as dedicated to NFL football as their husbands—giving it their time, their hearts, and their souls—but for all women it has become a way of life. Some women to whom I spoke said they struggled with their sense of identity after retirement, and some had to recognize that, even more than they realized, they'd grown accustomed to the prestige and attention.

One wife said, "I never knew that I liked the limelight, but whenever my husband and I went out, we never had to wait on a table, and we never had to wait in line for anything. Now, sometimes we have to wait. Well, if I have to stand in a line, I won't go. You get used to a certain way of living. When your husband retires, you are a commoner, and you miss the perks."

Many of the wives to whom I spoke said they felt isolated in retirement. They could talk to few people about their retirement-related troubles. Family and nonfootball friends could be empathetic, but they could not understand or identify with what they were experiencing. Women also said that people outside football continued to watch and judge. Sometimes it seemed that people were even waiting for their husbands or their marriages to falter, giving NFL women another reason to keep their problems quiet.

Retired NFL women also felt cut off from women on their husbands' former teams. After retirement, they were no longer invited to NFL get-togethers and were generally excluded from their former circles of NFL wives. Some women said they felt as though they no longer had anything in common with their recently lost NFL friends. They certainly didn't feel comfortable discussing their myriad retirement-related concerns with women whose husbands were still in the league.

Back to Work

Several current NFL women told me they planned to start a business or return to their jobs after their partners retired. But how feasible is this? As the multitude of women who have taken time off to raise their children can attest, the business world waits for no one. With an outdated resume and sub-par technical skills, retired women said that reassimilation into the workforce was far from easy. Extra schooling and additional credentials were often needed to catch up.

One obstacle that deters some women from going back to work is their husbands' poor physical condition. Though the league disputes the claim that retired NFL players have a shorter life expectancy than the average male, nearly everyone leaves pro football with some sort of injury. Some unfortunate women begin a back-breaking, physically grueling job in NFL retirement—as their husbands' caregivers. Even retired coaches encounter serious health problems (such as heart disease), which are brought on by their excruciatingly long hours and stressful seasons. In one retired marriage, the wife has to pull socks over her former linebacker husband's feet because he cannot bend over to do it himself.

Even if a retired player's or coach's body is intact, chances are his emotions are not. Considering their husbands' increased neediness and fragile mental condition, some women said they would feel guilty leaving them at home while they entered the work world. As one woman says, "How was I going to go off and start an exciting new job when he was still getting over losing his?"

Despite the numerous and valid difficulties they faced after their partners' retirement, a significant number of NFL women believed, as Susan May found out, that adjusting to life without football would have been easier if they had maintained a career. Not only would a job have meant a financial contribution, but the women also felt they would have been less disillusioned and less insecure in NFL retirement if their focus throughout the years had not always been on their partners and *their* jobs. They said their retired lives would not feel as empty if they had had their own thing going on, separate from football.

One retired linebacker's wife voiced such regrets. She says, "The wives in Jacksonville, many of them had jobs. I thought they were crazy. Why would they work? Now, I think back on how much time I wasted in those ten years. My whole week revolved around Sunday football games, deciding what to wear, making arrangements for the kids, whatever. I could have actually been doing something worthwhile, something for me, because now, here I am . . . and I don't know what to do."

One woman, speaking of her husband, voiced the sentiments of every retired wife to whom I spoke, and her comment in some ways applies to the women as well: "Football is still in him. He didn't go out the way he wanted to. If you don't go out on your own terms, you've still got a little bit left in you that you want to get out."

In the NFL, the end often comes too soon, and no matter how hard the life has been, most voice regrets when it's over. Those who lead the fullest and most varied lives during their NFL tenure seem to adjust best once it's finished, but few would deny wanting one more chance to shine.

When I asked Jackie Rice if she will miss the NFL when her husband retires, she did not hesitate. "Definitely," she says. "I can't say that I won't because, you know, I just grew up on it. I got started with it early, my kids got started with it early, and we grew up on the NFL. The day at the ballpark on Sundays for my kids — they love it. During the off-season, we kind of go through a little withdrawal: 'Ho hum, what are we going to do on Sunday?' We will miss it."

EPILOGUE Where Are They Now?

Chandra and Dwight Hollier

Chandra and Dwight currently live in Albemarle, North Carolina. Chandra is an OB/GYN with a medical practice in town, and she is considering becoming a partner. Chandra says, "I really love the practice that I am with."

A former linebacker, Dwight left the NFL in 2002 after being cut by the Indianapolis Colts at the end of training camp. Though he at first decided to pursue a second career as a mental health counselor, the call of the gridiron is pulling him back toward football.

Chandra says, "Dwight is a volunteer coach with a local high school team, and he is quite active with the NFL Alumni. I am sure that he is quite used to not playing, but since he got a taste of being on the sidelines in a different capacity, I really think that he would like to pursue a coaching or player programs position."

Not surprisingly, Chandra says that "my advice to any wife—married to a professional athlete or not—is simply to complete the course of education toward the goals that you had before you met him. Sure, there may be delays because of moves, children, and so on, but do it. You will always know that if you need to work, you can, and it will be something that you enjoy doing. Also, it just feels awesome to accomplish your goals, and you should not have to give them up just because you marry someone. I absolutely *love* what I do, everything about it, and that makes such a difference."

Pat and Larry Kennan

Pat says that "life is very good these days. We've actually lived in Virginia for three years now. That's a long time for us, and it's neat to have a sense of my surroundings. For instance, when we went to vote today, I knew exactly where to go."

Pat's husband, Larry, is currently the executive director of the NFLCA, and their three sons (who are described in chapter 7) are "all grown" and out of the house, so Pat says, "I keep busy with a variety of things — taking care of our two Old English sheepdogs and fostering an occasional Old English sheepdog. I also do volunteer work connected with alcohol and substance abuse."

Gina and Joe Nedney

Gina's husband, Joe, is a place-kicker currently in the final year of a five-year contract with the Tennessee Titans, and the couple is anticipating that if he doesn't sign another contract with the Titans in 2005, he will be playing somewhere in the NFL for at least another couple of years.

Gina jokes that her current job is "Full-Time Research Analyst in Human Relations and Development, a.k.a. being a mom." In June 2002, the Nedneys welcomed their first child into the world, a daughter, Gabrielle. Gina says that she is "still a certified occupational therapist for the state of Tennessee, but I am currently enjoying my roles as mom, wife, and caretaker of the Nedney B&B. We have company staying at our house fourteen out of sixteen weekends during the season. That is a lot of cleaning, shopping, and entertaining."

One senses, however, that it's mainly the company of her daughter that keeps Gina home. Gina says, "She makes me laugh every day. She is the best thing to happen to our lives. Children are such a blessing."

Julianne and Scott Player

Julianne comments, "I am thrilled to say that we are still living in Arizona! Scott has just started his seventh season with the Arizona

Cardinals. We feel very fortunate to have had a job in one place for this amount of time. The biggest change in our lives has been the addition of our two little girls, born in 2000 and 2001. They are amazing little people. They have stolen our hearts, and we have been blessed. I am fortunate enough to be able to stay home with our girls. It is the toughest and most rewarding job I have ever had."

In addition, Julianne has been working as a volunteer with other NFL wives for the Pat Tillman Foundation, a charitable organization that was created "to carry forward Pat's legacy by inspiring people to make positive changes in themselves and the world around them through the implementation of educational programs." Pat Tillman was a former Arizona Cardinal and a U.S. Army Ranger who was killed in Afghanistan in 2004 while serving in Operation Enduring Freedom.

Jackie and Jerry Rice

After spending four seasons with the Oakland Raiders, Jerry was traded to Seattle in the middle of the 2004 season. Then, in August 2005, after attending training camp with the Denver Broncos, the forty-three-year-old wide receiver—or, as he is known, the GOAT (the Greatest Of All Time)—decided to retire. The family maintains its longtime home in the San Francisco Bay Area, and Jackie and Jerry have already started a few business ventures, one of which is their own entertainment company, JJR Entertainment (Jacqueline and Jerry Rice Entertainment). The company has begun signing artists, the first of whom was their own seventeen-year-old daughter, who is a singer. The couple is also involved in numerous charities, such as the Jerry Rice 127 foundation, the March of Dimes, the Big Brothers and Big Sisters of the Peninsula, the Omega Boys Club, the United Negro College Fund, and Students Rising Above, which is an organization that helps underprivileged kids go to college and attend to their needs. Of their charitable work, Jackie says, "We help out when we can. If you can't help anyone else, what good is it to have any of it?"

Asked what piece of advice she would give to a new NFL woman, Jackie replies, "You kind of stay real by pulling yourself away from the limelight. We are very blessed to have a beautiful house and nice cars, but we have never been into the party scene with the entourage." The thought of it makes Jackie laugh. "Our entourage is our family when they come out to visit."

Kim and Tim Ruddy

At the end of the 2003 season, after ten years of professional football, Tim Ruddy made the decision to retire. After first deliberating with Kim and his children, he declined signing a contract with the New England Patriots.

By all accounts, the Ruddy family made exactly the right decision. Almost immediately the family bought a luxury RV, and within three months they had visited sixteen states. Traveling together and seeing the country has made the family "that much closer," says Kim, though Kim says she and Tim get more than a few strange looks from the much older, retired RV crowd.

Typical of linemen, Tim has lost the upwards of fifty pounds required for his position, and despite the need for "one more shoulder surgery," he is feeling great. For several years Tim has been a financial adviser in the off-season and he has stepped up his work, so he is now busy nearly full-time out of his home office.

At first, Kim said, retirement felt like an "extended off-season," and it was hard to get used to having Tim around. But now she couldn't be enjoying it more. Most important, Tim no longer spends evenings stressed out studying for an upcoming game; he doesn't care anymore about what is going to happen next week if the team loses. Plus, the man she loves no longer aches constantly with game-inflicted soreness and discomfort. The couple can now stroll through the neighborhood or walk from a parking lot to a movie theater without Tim grimacing in pain.

Kim and Tim both are taking more active roles in their children's activities. They take turns driving their children to school in the morning, and they are leader and co-leader of their six-year-old daughter's Brownie troop and their eight-year-old son's Boy Scout troop.

Kim is also entertaining thoughts about reentering the tennis world. She has begun training and getting back into shape, but with children in grade school, she knows the motherhood-to-career transition will be a slow one.

Kim and Mike Singletary

After ten years away from football, Mike joined the Baltimore Ravens in 2002 as a linebacker coach. Then in January 2005 the Hall of Famer became the assistant head coach/linebackers coach for the San Francisco 49ers. (Mike Nolan, Kathy's husband, was named the 49ers' head coach in 2005.) Kim says that she is happy Mike is coaching, but for the couple as well as for their seven children it remains an adjustment. No one, Mike included, likes the long hours, but they enjoy having the excitement of the NFL back in their lives.

Kim says she's happy Mike is coaching mainly because "his mind was too energetic, and it was all involving me somehow. We are very close, and he wants me to participate in *everything*. I was participating in new business ventures. I was participating in new houses. His mind stays very creative; he needed an outlet for that. Coaching is perfect because every week there is a new challenge, a new game. And I am not involved." Kim laughs. "All of his energy stays there, and when he is home, he is truly like, 'Oh this is nice. I need to sit down and chill out.' It works really nicely."

I asked Kim to reflect on the difficulties and positives of being an interracial couple in the high-profile NFL, and she said, "I feel like God really blessed us with a platform by having Mike and me in the public eye; it opened doors that would have been closed. Then, once we were in those doors, I can't tell you how many times people have said, 'I was always prejudiced, but you two really changed my perspective.' And that is what I really think God did. Also our kids have grown up never knowing prejudice. They have friends from black families and white families. For the twenty years we spent in Chicago, we didn't have family there. We had this huge group of friends, and they were our family for holidays and birthdays. My kids have never known any other way. All the races are represented, and everybody is friends."

Lori and George Warhop

George is currently in his second season as the offensive line coach for the Dallas Cowboys. The couple has an eight-year-old daughter, Olivia, and a seven-year-old son, Jacob, and they are enjoying living in Texas.

Lori says, "Because we move frequently, our family philosophy is 'When in Rome . . . .' The kids are taking horseback riding lessons and loving it. I am volunteering a lot at their school, and I also have written several children's stories that I hope to get published." The busy mom continues, "My girlfriend and I have a patent on a hair care product that would be used in salons, and I am working on a couple of other ideas for patents that I am trying to make prototypes for and get to market." In other words, look for Lori on your cable station's home shopping or decorating shows in the near future!

Kathy and Mike Waufle

After six years as a position coach with the Oakland Raiders, Mike and the team parted ways in 2003, after a particularly disappointing season. But within days the New York Giants signed Mike to a multiyear contract to coach their defensive line. Mike and Kathy now live only three hours from their families' hometown in upstate New York, and Kathy strongly believes she and Mike have come full circle. "We knew we would end up back home someday," she says. "It was meant to be." Nevertheless, Kathy is ambivalent. She is happy to be closer to family but says she misses the friends she made on the West Coast.

An NFL woman has to find consolation where she can. Kathy admits, "After being a Raider's wife and becoming a Giant's wife, I have had a great excuse to buy some new clothing. My wardrobe has gone from black to red, white, and blue."

Shannon O'Toole and John Morton

After seven faithful seasons coaching for the Oakland Raiders, in January 2005 John was informed by the head coach that his contract would not be renewed. Despite the Raiders' dismal season, considering John's long history with the Silver and Black, the firing was still a surprise. After an exhaustive job hunt John came to the realization that he would not be on the NFL sidelines next season. According to Shannon, "Even though we've been through an NFL firing when John was a player and I knew from my many interviews with other coaches' wives that this time was inevitable, when he didn't get another job right away, it was extremely stressful.

The worry over our future caused sleepless nights and a lot of strain in our relationship."

Attitude truly is everything, and after a while, the couple hit a turning point. Shannon and John decided not to worry about what would or would not happen with football. Instead, they decided to count their many blessings and to take advantage of John's time off. They have taken family day trips to the beach and gone on relaxing afternoon bike rides. John finds his peace in two-to-three-hour trail hikes, and he and Shannon cook dinner together every night (OK, John does the cooking). John misses football for sure, but there is no doubt that sitting out has been excellent for his health. He has lost twenty-five pounds, and his cholesterol level has dropped significantly. The past several months spent together have formed an incredibly close bond between father and daughter.

"Football is important," says Shannon. "It is our family's livelihood, but taking a step back (even if it's forced) from any demanding, all-consuming job can actually be a good thing. John's firing by the Raiders has reinforced for both of us that John, Tierney, and I are on the same team." "And after all," Shannon concludes, "What doesn't kill us. . . ."

APPENDIX The League's Role

Numerous NFL women with whom I spoke believed that the league could help improve their experiences by offering formal assistance that would help meet the unique needs of NFL women. Several teams have attempted to organize wives' groups and associations within their individual clubs, but their grassroots ideas often wane and fizzle. Similar to the mandatory rookie symposium, the league should organize a set of programs geared to the wives, girlfriends, and significant others of NFL players and coaches. This appendix is a brief description of what these programs could entail.

The NFL Rookie Symposium, now in its eighth year, is required for the entire rookie draft class. The four-day symposium includes presentations, videos, and workshops on subjects such as personal finance, life skills, personal conduct, life as a rookie, media policy, substance abuse, family issues, player development, and handling success in the NFL, as well as life after the NFL.

At a minimum, the league should organize a similar symposium for women. Held either during training camp, when the players and coaches are away from home, or during a four-day weekend during the off-season, such a conference or symposium would provide both practical information on a wide range of topics and a social setting that currently does not exist where NFL women can meet outside of the confines of game day and the parameters of their husbands' particular jobs. Possible program topics should include the following (to name just a few): raising NFL kids, money management, self-identity issues, ways to cope with game-day stress, dealing with a partner's injuries and workplace pressures, and overcoming the devastation and powerlessness when a partner loses his job.

Though the topic of safe sex is discussed at the rookie symposium, league representatives should also ensure that NFL women are actively included in discussions regarding sexual diseases. After all, they are most often the innocent bystanders of this problem. It may be uncomfortable to talk about the consequences of sex outside of marriage, but the risk of contracting HIV should override everything. Former basketball superstar and HIV-positive Magic Johnson and his wife would likely agree.

Unlike the rookie symposium, from which lesser-known free agent players are excluded, the women's symposium should encompass every NFL woman: from the newly pregnant girlfriend of a practice squad running back, to the wife of a low-profile veteran lineman, to the mother of three and the wife of an ever-mobile assistant position coach. The subjects discussed should include valuable information for every NFL lifestyle—as opposed to addressing only the typical concerns of high-profile superstar athletes and their families.

In addition, an annual NFL women's symposium would provide the opportunity for NFL women to share and listen to the stories of others in an open format, and this alone would help lessen the difficulties women inevitably face. The common and sometimes institutionally created divisions among NFL women (as we have seen in this book) might also be minimized, and women might have increased empathy for one another. For instance, players' and coaches' wives might learn about the challenges that each group faces, and this increased awareness might foster understanding, outreach, and even friendships. Both groups of women would glean a better understanding of how the league operates and what they can expect in the years ahead.

NFL husbands are notorious for failing to pass on pertinent information about the league to their wives. Even if they weren't, there is no reason not to actively inform women of league policies and programs. An NFL women's symposium would also be a good time to educate women on topics ranging from the newly implemented Fritz Pollard Alliance (which aims to create racial equity in the coaching ranks) to other practical and financial matters, such as adjustments to retirement benefits. As I have tried to show, women and families are as affected by NFL policies and procedures as their husbands. Numerous retired wives with whom I spoke regretted not staying more informed on issues such as these during their husbands' careers.

An offshoot of a women's symposium could be an NFL Women's Mentoring Program. Its mission would be to lessen the strain and uncertainty and thereby increase the life satisfaction of women new to the league by formally connecting them with experienced veteran wives. In these relationships, veteran NFL women would offer advice, answer questions, and guide their mentees in developing skills and methods to better cope with the myriad of circumstances unique to NFL life; mentees would benefit from their mentors' experience without having to go through the trial and error of learning the same lessons over the years.

A mentoring program is important because moving from team to team—as many players and the majority of assistant coaches do—increases women's social isolation. By not staying in one place for any significant amount of time, women are unable to cultivate close relationships or observe how other women deal with NFL-related issues. Without the trustworthy advice of a nonjudgmental friend (kinship is a process that occurs over time), some women have difficulty managing the major NFL life changes and decisions. Frequent mobility makes it difficult for women to gain group support, which is essential for fostering one's confidence and self-assurance.

Perhaps most important, the league needs to take a more proactive approach on the topic of interpersonal violence. The women in this book who spoke about violence involving NFL men are extremely brave individuals. Even if NFL players are not more prone toward domestic and gender violence than men outside of football, NFL representatives need to find ways to reach out and assist *any* NFL woman involved in a dysfunctional and dangerous relationship. Appropriate resources need to be made easily available to such a woman; these could include a telephone hotline or a web site for those seeking help.

This aggressive approach to the problem, along with the enforcement of a permanent ban for men convicted of a second violent offense, would send a clear message to professional football's abusers: violence toward women will not be tolerated.

Last, it is my belief, as well as that of numerous women with whom I spoke during the preparation of this book, that the league should find ways to honor and validate NFL women for the incredible sacrifices *they* make to the game. Although the NFL Pro Bowl Women's Luncheon has recently been organized for this purpose, a league-wide symposium would include more than the partners of high-profile players and winning coaches. Players and coaches are of course the game's participants, and they should and do have plenty of opportunities for acknowledgement, but it wouldn't take much to occasionally put the focus on the NFL's women and to recognize them for *their* accomplishments. Considering the increased responsibility that NFL relationships bear and the important role these women have in their husbands' lives and careers—and ultimately in the league—the NFL owes it to these women to make them feel special, even if it is just one weekend a year. With such efforts on the part of the NFL, women will finally begin to receive the recognition and support they so desperately deserve.